Hana's Suitcase Anniversary Album

by

Karen Levine

A TRUE STORY

Second Story Press

NATIONAL LIBRARY OF CANADA CATALOGUING IN PUBLICATION DATA

Levine, Karen, 1955-
Hana's suitcase anniversary album / by Karen Levine.

(A Holocaust remembrance series for young readers)
Issued also in electronic formats.
ISBN 978-1-926920-36-8

1. Levine, Karen, 1955- Hana's suitcase—Juvenile literature. 2. Levine, Karen, 1955- —
Appreciation—Juvenile literature. 3. Brady, Hana—Juvenile literature. 4. Jewish children in
the Holocaust—Juvenile literature. 5. Holocaust, Jewish (1939-1945), in literature—Juvenile
literature. I. Title. II. Series: Holocaust remembrance book for young readers

DS135.C97B732 2012   j940.53'18092   C2011-908647-6

Editor: Margie Wolfe
Copyeditors: Sarah Silberstein Swartz and Laura McCurdy
Design: Stephanie Martin and Melissa Kaita

Printed and bound in Canada

Document on page 73 from the Terezin Ghetto Museum. Reprinted with permission. Photo credits
for page 148 (clockwise): Lorraine Kimsa Theatre for Young People, Metro Theater Company/
Jerry Naunheim, The Grand Theatre. Photo credits for page 149 (clockwise): Kaleidoscope Theatre
Productions, Nephesh Theatre, Magnus Theatre Company, First Stage (left to right) Jessica
Schmeling, Pahoua Vang, Haruna Tsuchiya, Touly Vang (photo by Mark Frohna).

Please note: All student writing has been reproduced verbatim. The publisher has made every
effort to properly identify and credit students' work.

*Second Story Press would like to thank George Brady and his family for generously allowing us to use
his family photographs and documents in this book. We would also like to express our appreciation to
Fumiko Ishioka and the Holocaust Education Resource Center in Tokyo for sharing their photographs and
materials here as well. We are grateful to Ludmilla Chládková from the Terezin Ghetto Museum (which
rarely closes) for her on-going support.*

*For Hana's Suitcase Anniversary Album, the Author and the Publisher would like to especially
acknowledge the work of editor Kathryn Cole and book designer Melissa Kaita along with other Second
Story Press staff, Carolyn Jackson and Emma Rodgers. We would also like to thank Rona Ramon for
generously allowing us to use the excerpt from her late husband's diary and Sherry Norman for sharing
the beautiful story of her daughter Alicia and the quilts. We appreciate the contribution of so many
eduators, especially, Wendy Alexis, Ilyse Lustig, Shawntelle Nesbitt, and Diane Vey-Morawski. Fumiko
Ishioka, George and Lara Brady have been wonderful about sharing their photographs and letters. And
most importantly, we want to thank all the young people whose work is included and who continue to
learn from Hana's story and tell us how much the book means to them.*

*Second Story Press gratefully acknowledges the support of the Ontario Arts Council, the Ontario Media
Development Corporation, and the Canada Council for the Arts for our publishing program. We
acknowledge the financial support of the Government of Canada through the Canada Book Fund.*

Published by
SECOND STORY PRESS
20 Maud Street, Suite 401
Toronto, ON
M5V 2M5
www.secondstorypress.ca

ONTARIO ARTS COUNCIL
CONSEIL DES ARTS DE L'ONTARIO

Canada Council   Conseil des Arts
for the Arts   du Canada

For my parents,
Helen and Gil Levine.

Welcome to the Album

Everyone knew Hana's Suitcase *was a remarkable book when it was first published a decade ago, but no one could have guessed the dramatic impact it would have on readers of all ages in all parts of the world. Through this book, one humble, battered suitcase with a little girl's name on it has traveled farther than its owner could ever have imagined. It has become a symbol of hope, an ambassador of goodwill, and a reminder that acceptance and understanding are ultimately more powerful than tyranny and hatred.*

Now, at age ten, Hana's Suitcase *is in its twenty-eighth printing, is published in forty-five countries and has been the catalyst for stage and film dramatizations, prose, poetry, and every kind of exploration of the worst and best humanity has to offer. It has won national and international recognition, and holds the most awards of any Canadian children's book ever. Thanks to* Hana's Suitcase *and the perseverance of the amazing people behind it, the image of Hana Brady has become, as one young reader put it, the "face inside of everyone." She brings the one-and-a-half million children who died in the Holocaust into sharp focus.*

Contents

Foreword

The untimely death of anyone is always very sad but none more so than the death of a young person whose life is so filled with promise. There are many heart-wrenching stories of the loss of human potential which emerge from the tragedy of the Holocaust. *The Diary of Anne Frank* immediately comes to mind, but *Hana's Suitcase* bridges many worlds. It tells the remarkable and very moving story of how the curiosity of Japanese children inspires Fumiko Ishioka, a teacher at the Tokyo Holocaust Center, to embark in 2000, some fifty-five years after the Holocaust, on an epic search to give 'life' to a name which appears on a forlorn suitcase — one of the many thousands of confiscated suitcases found at the Auschwitz death camp.

How extraordinary that this humble suitcase has enabled children all over the world to learn through Hana's story the terrible history of what happened and that it continues to urge them to heed the warnings of history. Hana's story reminds us all to be constantly vigilant to inhumanity, predjudice, bigotry and the terrible consequences of silence, indifference, and apathy.

This book will be a useful tool for teachers in South Africa, who are teaching in classrooms that are so removed in time and space from the terrible events of the Holocaust. Nobody can easily grasp the persecution and deaths of millions of people. It is only through the personal stories that we can understand the extent of the tragedy. Hana came from an ordinary Jewish family and like any young girl she had modest hopes and dreams for her future. However that future was denied to her simply because of who she was, not because of anything that she or her parents had done. Young people here in South Africa will be able to identify with Hana's dreams and recognize the discriminatory laws passed against her family, their exclusion from society, her parents' incarceration, and having to assume adult responsibilities long before she should. All this will resonate with young South Africans as they learn about their own painful history. As we struggle with the challenges of building a new South Africa, this book helps to remind us that each person should be valued as being of infinite worth, irrespective of differences, and that, with that attitude, we will ultimately create a more caring and just society.

Hana wanted to become a teacher, and surely through this little book her dream is being realized.

+Archbishop Emeritus Desmond Tutu,
patron of the South African Holocaust Foundation

Introduction

Hana's Suitcase is a true story that takes place on three continents over a period of almost seventy years. It brings together the experiences of a girl and her family in Czechoslovakia in the 1930s and '40s, a young woman and a group of children in Tokyo, Japan, and a man in Toronto, Canada in modern times.

Between 1939 and 1945, the world was at war. Nazi dictator Adolf Hitler wanted Germany to rule the globe. At the center of his vision was the brutal elimination of the Jewish people from the face of the earth. To get rid of his "enemies," he set up dozens of prison camps — called concentration camps — across Europe. Jewish women, men and children from almost every country on the continent were deported; they were torn from their homes and sent to the camps, where they endured terrible suffering. Many people died of hunger and disease. Most were murdered. In these death camps and elsewhere — where Hitler's followers carried out his terrible plan — six million Jews were killed. One-and-a-half million Jewish children were among them.

In 1945, the war ended and the entire world learned the horrors of what had gone on in the concentration camps. Since then, people have been trying to understand more about what is today known as the "Holocaust," the worst example of mass murder — or genocide — in human history. How did it happen? How can we make sure it will never happen again?

In Japan, a country allied with Nazi Germany during the Second World War, attention to the history of the Holocaust is relatively new. An anonymous Japanese donor, who wanted to contribute to global tolerance and understanding, decided it was important for young people in Japan to learn more about this aspect of world history. Single-handedly, this donor has endowed the Tokyo Holocaust Education Resource Center, which is dedicated to that purpose.

At a Children's Forum on the Holocaust held in 1999, two hundred students from schools in the Tokyo area met Holocaust survivor Yaffa Eliach. She told them about how almost every Jew in her village, young and old, was murdered by the Nazis. At the end of her talk, she reminded her audience that children have the power "to create peace in the future." A dozen of the young Japanese people there took her challenge to heart and formed a group called "Small Wings." Now the members of Small Wings, aged eight to eighteen, meet every month. They publish a newsletter, help run the Tokyo Holocaust Education Resource Center and work to interest other Japanese children in the history of the Holocaust. They do their work under the guidance of Fumiko Ishioka, the director of the Tokyo Holocaust Center.

The suitcase — Hana's suitcase — is a key to the success of their mission. In it lies a story of terrible sadness and great joy, a reminder of the brutality of the past and of hope for the future.

Hana's Suitcase

Tokyo, Japan, Winter 2000

REALLY, IT'S A VERY ORDINARY LOOKING SUITCASE. A little tattered around the edges, but in good condition.

It's brown. It's big. You could fit quite a lot in it — clothes for a long trip, maybe. Books, games, treasures, toys. But there is nothing inside it now.

Every day children come to a little museum in Tokyo, Japan to see this suitcase. It sits in a glass cabinet. And through the glass you can see that there is writing on the suitcase. In white paint, across the front, there is a girl's name: Hana Brady. A date of birth: May 16, 1931. And one other word: *Waisenkind.* That's the German word for orphan.

The Japanese children know that the suitcase came from Auschwitz, a concentration camp where millions of people suffered and died during the Second World War between 1939 and 1945. But who was Hana Brady? Where did she come from? Where was she traveling to? What did she pack? How did she become an orphan? What kind of girl was she and what happened to her?

The children are full of questions. So is the director of the museum, a slender young woman with long black hair named Fumiko Ishioka.

Fumiko and the children gently take the suitcase out of the glass case and open it. They search the side pockets. Maybe Hana left something that would be a clue. Nothing. They look under the polka-dot lining. There are no hints there either.

Fumiko promises the children to do everything she can to find out about the girl who owned the suitcase, to solve the mystery. And for the next year, she becomes a detective, scouring the world for clues to the story of Hana Brady.

Hana's suitcase. Though she spelled her name with one "n," the German spelling has two, as on the suitcase.

3

The town of Nové Město na Moravě and its surroundings.

Nové Město na Moravě, Czechoslovakia, 1930s

IN ROLLING HILLS in the middle of what was then Czechoslovakia, in a province called Moravia, there was a town called Nové Město na Moravě. It wasn't big, but it was famous. And in the winter, especially, it was a very busy place. People from all over the country came to cross-country ski in Nové Město na Moravě. There were races to be raced. There were trails to be blazed and there were frozen ponds for skating. In the summer, there was swimming, sailing, fishing and camping.

Nové Město na Moravě was home to 4,000 people. Once the town was well known for making glass. But in the 1930s, people worked in the forests and in little workshops that made skis. On the main street, there was a large, two-story white building. It had a two-story attic. And in its basement, a secret passageway led to a church on the town's main square. In olden days, when the town was under siege, it was used by soldiers to store food and supplies for the people of Nové Město na Moravě.

The town's general store was on the ground floor. There, you could buy almost anything — buttons, jam, oil lamps and rakes, sleigh bells, stones for sharpening knives, dishes, paper and pens and candy. On the second floor lived the Brady family: father Karel, mother Marketa, Hana and her big brother George.

Father worked six days a week in the store. He was an athlete, known to almost everyone in Nové Město na Moravě for his love of soccer, skiing and gymnastics. He was also an amateur actor with a big booming voice that could be heard from one end of a playing field to the other. Because of this, Father was chosen to call the cross-country ski races over a megaphone, so that everyone could hear the action. He was a volunteer firefighter who, with other men from the town, rode the fire engine to help people in emergencies.

The Brady family opened its home to artists of all kinds — musicians, painters and poets, sculptors and actors. When they were hungry, they could always find a hot meal, produced by Boshka, the family housekeeper and cook. And their artistic talents found an eager audience, which, of course, included two impish children — Hana and George. Sometimes George was called upon to play his violin. Hana was more than willing to demonstrate her skill on the piano to anyone who would listen. And in the middle of the living room, there was a record player that was cranked up by hand. Hana played her favorite song — "I Have Nine Canaries" — over and over again.

Hana in costume for a school play.

Mother was a warm and generous hostess with a good sense of humor and a very loud laugh. She, too, worked six days a week in the store and people often came in just to hear her jokes and banter. She paid special attention to poor people in Nové Město na Moravě who lived on the outskirts of town. Once a week, she would prepare a bundle of food and clothing that Hana would deliver to needy neighbors. Hana was very proud of her mission and she pestered her mother to make care packages more often.

Hana was a helper in the store, too. From the time they were very small, Hana and George had the job of keeping the shelves stocked, clean and tidy. They learned how to slice

Nové Město na Moravě. The Brady family lived on the second floor of the fourth building from the left. Their store was on the main floor.

yeast, chisel small lumps off the sugar loaf, weigh spices and seasonings, and twist paper into the shape of hollow cones to be filled with candy and sold as treats. Once in a while, Mother noticed that some of those candy cones were missing. Hana never told on George. And he never told on Hana.

There were always cats around the store, who worked full-time as mouse catchers. But once, as a special surprise, Mother and Father ordered fluffy white angora kittens as pets for the children. Two soft little bundles arrived through the mail in a box with breathing holes. At first, Sylva, the family wolfhound, a huge, gray, furry creature, sniffed around them suspiciously. But soon the kittens, who Hana named Micki and Mourek, became accepted members of the family.

Hana and George went to the public school. They were average kids, who got into regular mischief and had the usual problems and triumphs. There was just one thing that was different about them.

The Bradys were Jewish. They weren't a religious family. But Mother and Father wanted the children to know about their heritage. Once a week, while their playmates were at church, Hana and George sat with a special teacher who taught them about Jewish holidays and Jewish history.

There were a few other Jewish families in Nové Město na Moravě. But Hana and George were the only Jewish children in the town. In their early years no one really noticed or cared that they were different. Soon, though, the fact that they were Jews would become the most important thing about them.

Tokyo, Winter 2000

BACK IN HER OFFICE, half a world away in Japan and more than half a century later, Fumiko Ishioka remembered how the suitcase had come to her.

In 1998, she had begun her job as coordinator of a small museum, called the Tokyo Holocaust Center. It was dedicated to teaching Japanese children about the Holocaust. At a conference in Israel, Fumiko had met a few Holocaust survivors, people who had lived through the horrors of the concentration camps. She was astonished by their optimism and their joy in living, despite everything they had been through. When Fumiko felt sad about things in her own life, she often thought about these survivors. They were so strong-willed and wise. They had so much to teach her.

Fumiko wanted young people in Japan to learn from the Holocaust as well. It was her job to make it happen. And it wasn't an easy one. How, she wondered, could she help Japanese children understand the terrible story of what

Fumiko teaching children at the Center about the Holocaust.

happened to millions of Jewish children on a faraway continent over fifty years ago?

She decided the best way to start would be through physical objects that the children could see and touch. She wrote to Jewish and Holocaust museums all over the world — in Poland, Germany, the United States and Israel — asking for a loan of artifacts that had belonged to children. She posted her request on the Internet. She wrote to individuals she thought might be able to help. Fumiko was looking for a pair of shoes and for a suitcase.

Everyone turned her down, telling her that the objects they had so carefully preserved were too precious to send to such a small museum, so far away. Fumiko wasn't sure what to do next. But she wasn't the kind of person who gave up easily. Just the opposite. The more rejections she got, the more dedicated she became.

That fall, Fumiko traveled to Poland where many Nazi concentration camps had been located. There, on the site of the most well-known camp, she visited the Auschwitz Museum. Fumiko begged for a short meeting with the Museum's assistant director. She was given five minutes to explain what she wanted. When she left the assistant director's office, she had a promise that her request would be considered.

A few months later, a package from the Auschwitz Museum arrived: a child's sock and shoe, a child's sweater, a can of Zyklon B poisonous gas and one suitcase — Hana's suitcase.

The Holocaust Education Resource Center in Tokyo, Japan.

Fumiko Ishioka and one of the children visiting the Center.

Hana loved to play outdoors when she was young.

Nové Město na Moravě, 1938

HANA HAD BLONDE HAIR, blue eyes and a very pretty round face. She was a strong girl. Once in a while, Hana would provoke a battle with George, just to show off her muscles. Even though her brother was three years older, Hana would sometimes emerge the winner. But most of the time, Hana and George played well together.

In the summer, in the creek behind their house, they pretended to be in the navy. Climbing into an old wooden washtub, the children sailed along until one or the other pulled the plug in the middle and they sank, laughing and splashing. There were three different kinds of swings in the backyard meadow — one for a small child, a two-seater, and one that swung from a giant tree out over the creek. Sometimes, the neighborhood children would gather there for swinging contests. Who could swing the highest? Who could jump the farthest? Often it was Hana.

In the long halls of their apartment over the store, Hana

The children building a snow fort.

raced on her red scooter, George on his blue one. In the winter, Hana and George built snow forts and skied. But Hana's greatest love was skating, and she worked hard perfecting her pirouettes on Nové Město na Moravě's frozen pond. Sometimes, when she wore her special red skating outfit — the one with the white fur on the ends of the sleeves — she imagined herself a dancing princess. Her parents, her friends and her brother applauded both the performance and the dream.

Because her parents worked six days a week, Sunday mornings were special for the family. When they woke up, George and Hana would snuggle up in their parents' bed under the fluffy feather comforter. On Sunday afternoons in the summer, they would all pile into the car and head off to the nearest fort or castle for a picnic, sometimes with Uncle Ludvik and Aunt Heda who also lived in Nové Město na Moravě. In the winter, there were sleigh

Hana in her special red skating outfit.

rides and long cross-country skiing adventures. Hana was a very strong skier. On the eight-kilometer run between Nové Město na Moravě and a nearby village (which had a wonderful tearoom with delicious creamy pastries), Hana always led the big family pack of cousins, even though she was the youngest.

Both Hana and George learned to ski when they were very young.

But by New Year's Eve 1938, there was a new and menacing feeling in the air. There was talk of war. Adolf Hitler and his Nazis were in power in Germany. Earlier that year, Hitler had taken over Austria. Then he had marched his armies into parts of Czechoslovakia. Refugees — people trying to escape the Nazis — started appearing at the Bradys' door, asking for money, food and shelter. They always found a warm welcome from Mother and Father. But the children were mystified. Who are these people? Hana wondered. Why are they coming here? Why don't they want to stay in their own homes?

In the evenings, after Hana and George had been sent to bed, Mother and Father would sit by the radio and listen to the news. Often friends came and joined them, and they would talk long into the night about the news they had heard. "We'll keep our voices down," they would say, "so as not to wake the children."

The conversation of the adults was so intense, the discussions so heated, that they rarely heard the squeak of floorboards in the darkened hall, as Hana and George tiptoed to their secret listening post just outside the living room. The children heard the talk about the new anti-Jewish laws in Austria. They heard about *Kristallnacht* in Germany, when gangs of Nazi thugs roamed through Jewish neighborhoods, breaking windows in homes and stores, burning synagogues, and beating people in the streets.

"It couldn't happen here, could it?" Hana whispered to her brother.

"Shhhh," said George. "If we talk now, they'll hear us and we'll be sent back to bed."

One night, their neighbor Mr. Rott presented a shocking idea to the adults. "We can all feel that a war is coming," he began. "It's not safe for Jews to be here. We should all leave Nové Město na Moravě, leave Czechoslovakia, for America, for Palestine, for Canada. For anywhere. Leave now, before it's too late."

The rest of the group was taken aback. "Are you crazy, Mr. Rott?" one asked. "This is our home. This is where we belong." And that settled that.

Despite the bad times, the Bradys were determined to celebrate the coming of 1939. On New Year's Eve, after a feast of turkey, sausage, salami and pudding, the children got ready to play the traditional game of predicting the future. Hana, George, and their young cousins from nearby towns were given half a walnut into which they each wedged a small candle. A large basin of water was dragged into the middle of the room. Each child launched a little walnut boat into it. Eleven-year-old George's boat wobbled in the water, turned round and round, and finally came to a stop, lopsided. His candle kept burning. Eight-year-old Hana launched hers and, for a moment, it glided along without a quiver. Then it shook, turned on its side, and the candle hit the water and went out.

Tokyo,
March 2000

FROM THE DAY THE SUITCASE arrived in Tokyo, Fumiko and the children were drawn to it. Ten-year-old Akira, who usually loved to joke and tease, wondered aloud what it would be like to be an orphan. Maiko, who was older, loved to party and was an accomplished synchronized swimmer. She always became very quiet in the presence of the suitcase. It made her think about being sent away from her own friends.

The suitcase was the only object they had at the Center that was linked to a name. From the date on the suitcase, Fumiko and the children figured out that Hana would have been thirteen years old when she was sent to Auschwitz. A year younger than me, said one girl. Just as old as my big sister, said Akira.

Fumiko wrote back to the Auschwitz Museum. Could they help her find out anything about the girl who owned the suitcase? No, they replied. They knew no more than she did. Fumiko reported back to the children. "Try somewhere else,"

Maiko urged. "Don't give up," said Akira. The kids chanted encouragement like a chorus: "Keep on looking." Fumiko promised to do just that.

Fumiko wrote to Yad Vashem, Israel's Holocaust museum. No, we have never heard of a girl named Hana Brady, the director wrote. Have you tried the Holocaust Memorial Museum in Washington, DC? Fumiko rushed a letter off to Washington, but the reply was the same. We have no information about a girl named Hana Brady. How discouraging it was!

Then, out of the blue, Fumiko received a note from the museum at Auschwitz. They had discovered something. They had found Hana's name on a list. It showed that Hana had come to Auschwitz from a place called Theresienstadt.

Nové Město na Moravě, 1939

ON MARCH 15, 1939, Hitler's Nazi troops marched into the rest of Czechoslovakia and the Brady family's life was changed forever. The Nazis declared that Jews were evil, a bad influence, dangerous. From now on, the Brady family and the other Jews in Nové Město na Moravě would have to live by different rules.

Jews could only leave their houses at certain hours of the day. They could only shop in certain stores and only at certain times. Jews weren't allowed to travel, so there were no more visits to beloved aunts, uncles, and grandmothers in nearby towns. The Bradys were forced to tell the Nazis about everything they owned — art, jewelery, cutlery, bank books. They hurriedly stashed their most precious papers in the ceiling of the attic. Father's stamp collection and Mother's silver were hidden with gentiles, non-Jewish friends. But the family radio had to be taken to a central office and surrendered to a Nazi official.

Hana and George stood by each other as the Nazi restrictions increased.

One day, Hana and George lined up at the movie theater to see *Snow White and the Seven Dwarfs*. When they got to the ticket box they saw a sign that read "No Jews Allowed." Their faces red, their eyes burning, Hana and George turned on their heels and headed for home. When Hana walked in the door, she was furious and very upset. "What is happening to us? Why can't I go to the movies? Why can't I just ignore the sign?" Mother and Father looked grimly at each other. There were no easy answers.

Every week seemed to bring a new restriction. No Jews in the playground. No Jews on the sports fields. No Jews in the parks. Soon Hana could no longer go to the gym. Even the skating pond was declared off limits. Her friends — all of them gentiles — at first were as mystified by the rules as Hana. They sat together in school as they always had, and still had good times making mischief in the classroom and in private backyards. "We'll be together forever, no matter what," promised Hana's best friend Maria. "We're not going to let anyone tell us who we can play with!"

A young Hana and her father.

But gradually, as the months dragged on, all Hana's playmates, even Maria, stopped coming over after school and on the weekends. Maria's parents had ordered her to stay away from Hana. They were afraid the Nazis would punish their whole family for allowing Maria to be friends with a Jewish child. Hana was terribly lonely.

With each loss of friendship and with each new restriction, Hana and George felt their world grow a little smaller. They were angry. They were sad. And they were frustrated. "What can we do?" they asked their parents. "Where can we go now?"

Mother and Father tried their best to distract the children, to help them find new ways to have fun. "We are lucky," Mother told them, "because we have such a big garden. You can play hide-and-seek. You can swing from the trees. You can invent games. You can play detective in the storerooms. You can explore the secret tunnel. You can play charades. Be grateful that you have each other!"

Hana and George were grateful to have each other and they did play together, but it didn't make them feel any better about all the things they couldn't do anymore, all the places they couldn't go. On a fine spring day, when the sun was shining, the two of them sat in the meadow, bored, fiddling with the grass. Suddenly Hana burst into tears. "It's not fair," she cried. "I hate this. I want it to be like it was before." She yanked a fistful of grass out of the ground and threw it in the air. She looked at her brother. She knew he was as miserable as she was. "Wait here," he said. "I have an idea." In minutes he was back, carrying a pad of paper, a pen, an empty bottle and a shovel.

"What's all that for?" Hana asked.

"Maybe if we write down all the things that are bothering us," he said, "it'll help us feel better."

"That's stupid," Hana replied. "It won't bring back the park or the playground. It won't bring back Maria."

But George insisted. He was, after all, the big brother, and Hana didn't have a better idea. And so for the next several hours, the children poured their unhappiness onto paper, with George doing most of the writing and Hana doing much of the talking. They made lists of things they missed, lists of things they were angry about. Then they made lists of all the things they would do, all the things they would have, and all the places they would go when these dark times were over.

When they were done, George took the sheets of paper, rolled them into a tube, stuffed them into the bottle and popped in the cork. Then the two of them walked back toward the house, stopping at the double swing. There, Hana dug a big hole. This would be a hiding place for some of their sadness and frustration. George placed the bottle at the bottom of the hole and Hana filled the space back up with earth. And when it was all over the world seemed a little lighter and brighter, at least for the day.

It was hard to make sense of everything that was happening. Especially now that the family radio was gone. Father and Mother had depended on hearing the eight o'clock news every night from London, England to keep them informed of Hitler's latest evil act. But Jews had been ordered inside their houses by eight. Listening to the radio was absolutely forbidden and the penalty for breaking any law was very severe. Everyone was afraid of being arrested.

Father hatched a plan, an ingenious way to get around the Nazi rules. He asked his old friend, the keeper of the big church clock, to do him a favor. Would he mind, Father asked, turning the clock back fifteen minutes in the early evenings? That way Father could rush to the neighbor's house, hear the news, and be safely home when the bell rang at eight (which was actually eight-fifteen). The Nazi guard who patrolled the town square didn't have a clue. And Father was thrilled that his scheme had worked. Unfortunately, the news he was able to hear on the radio was bad. Very bad. The Nazis were winning every battle, advancing on every front.

Hana and George.

Tokyo, March 2000

THERESIENSTADT. Now Fumiko and the children knew that Hana had come to Auschwitz from Theresienstadt. Fumiko was excited. This was the first solid piece of information she had found about Hana. The first clue.

Theresienstadt was the name that the Nazis gave to the Czech town of Terezin. It was a pretty little town, with two imposing fortresses, first built in the 1800s to hold military and political prisoners. After the Nazis invaded Czechoslovakia, they turned Terezin into the Theresienstadt ghetto — a walled, guarded, overcrowded prison town to hold Jews who had been forced to leave their homes. Over the course of World War II, more than 140,000 Jews were sent here — 15,000 of them were children.

Fumiko stayed up late at night, her office a glow of light in the darkened Center, reading everything she could find about Theresienstadt.

She learned that terrible things had happened in Theresienstadt, and that over the course of a few years almost everyone in the ghetto was deported again, put on trains and sent off to the more terrible concentration camps in the east which were known to be death camps.

But Fumiko also learned that brave and inspiring things happened in Theresienstadt. Among the adults were some very special people — great artists, famous musicians, historians, philosophers, fashion designers, social workers. They were all in Theresienstadt because they were Jews. An astonishing amount of talent, training and knowledge was crowded inside the walls of the ghetto. Under the noses of the Nazis and at great risk, the inmates secretly plotted and established an elaborate schedule of teaching, learning, producing and performing for both adults and children. They were determined to remind their students that — despite the war, despite the drab, cramped surroundings, despite everything — the world was a place of beauty and every person could add to it.

Fumiko also discovered that children in Theresienstadt were taught to paint and draw. And, miraculously, 4,500 drawings created by these children had survived the war. Fumiko's heart began to beat more quickly. Could it be that among those drawings there might be one or more by Hana Brady?

Nové Město na Moravě, Autumn 1940– Spring 1941

AUTUMN BROUGHT WITH IT A CHILL IN THE AIR, as well as more restrictions, and hardship.

Hana was about to begin grade three, when the Nazis announced that Jewish children would no longer be allowed to go to school. "Now, I will never see my friends!" Hana wailed, when her parents told her the bad news. "Now, I'll never become a teacher when I grow up!" She had always dreamed of standing up at the front of the classroom and having everyone listen carefully to whatever she had to say.

Mother and Father were determined that both Hana and her brother would continue their education. Luckily, they had enough money to hire a young woman from the next village to be Hana's tutor, and an old refugee professor to teach George.

Mother tried to be cheerful. "Good morning, Hana," she would sing out when the sun rose. "It's time for breakfast.

You don't want to be late for 'school.'" Every morning, Hana would meet her new tutor at the dining room table. She was a kind young woman and she did her best to encourage Hana with reading, writing and arithmetic. She brought a small blackboard that she leaned up against a chair. Once in a while, she allowed Hana to draw with the chalk and bang out chalk dust in the brushes. But at this school, there were no playmates, no practical jokes, no recess. Hana found it harder to pay attention or stay focused on her lessons. In the darkness of the winter, the world seemed to be closing in on the Brady family.

Indeed, when spring came, disaster struck. In March 1941, Mother was arrested by the Gestapo, Hitler's feared secret state police.

A letter came to the house ordering Mother to appear at nine o'clock in the morning at Gestapo headquarters in the nearby town of Iglau. In order to be there on time, she would have to leave in the middle of the night. She had one day to organize everything and say good-bye to her family.

She called Hana and George into the living room, sat on the couch, and pulled the children close to her. She told them that she would be going away for a while. Hana snuggled a little closer. "You must be good while I am gone," she said. "Listen carefully to Father and obey him. I will write," she promised. "Will you write back to me?"

George looked away. Hana trembled. The children were too shocked to reply. Their mother had never left them before.

Hana, her mother and George in happier times.

When Mother tucked Hana into bed that night, she held her tightly. Mother ran her soothing fingers through Hana's hair, just the way she had when Hana was very little. She sang Hana's favorite lullaby, over and over again. Hana fell asleep with her arms around her mother's neck. In the morning when Hana woke up, Mother was gone.

Tokyo, April 2000

FUMIKO COULD HARDLY BELIEVE IT when a flat package arrived at her office in Tokyo. Just a few weeks earlier, she had written to the Terezin Ghetto Museum in what is now called the Czech Republic. Fumiko had explained in her letter how anxious she and the children were to find anything that would connect them more closely to Hana. People there said they knew nothing about Hana's personal story. But they did know about the huge collection of children's drawings that had been hidden in the camp. Many of the drawings were now displayed at the Jewish Museum in Prague.

Fumiko opened the package. She was so excited that her hands were shaking. There were photographs of five drawings. One was a colored drawing of a garden and a park bench. Another showed people having a picnic beside a river. The rest were in pencil and charcoal, one of a tree, another of farmhands drying hay in a field, and another of stick people carrying suitcases, getting off a train. In the top right hand corner of each of the drawings was the name "Hana Brady."

One of Hana's drawings from Theresienstadt.

Nové Město na Moravě, Spring– Autumn 1941

SINCE SHE HAD MADE A PROMISE TO HER MOTHER, Hana did her best to behave well. She helped her father when she could and did her lessons. Boshka, their much-loved housekeeper, tried to cook Hana's favorite meals and give her extra helpings of dessert. But Hana missed her mother terribly, especially at night. No one else could smooth her hair with quite the same touch. No one else could sing her lullaby. And that big booming laugh of her mother's — everyone missed that.

The children learned that their mother was in a place called Ravensbruck, a women's concentration camp in Germany. "Is it far away?" Hana asked her father.

"When is she coming home?" George wanted to know. Father assured the children that he was doing everything he could to get her out.

One day Hana was reading in her room when she heard Boshka calling for her. She decided to ignore her. Hana didn't feel like doing any chores. And what else was there to look forward to? But Boshka kept calling. "Hana, Hana? Where are you? Come quickly! There is something very special waiting for you at the post office."

When she heard that, Hana dropped her book. Could it be what she hoped for most? She burst out of the house and ran down the street to the post office. Hana approached the wicket. "Do you have something for me?" she asked. The woman behind the counter slid a small brown package through the hole. Hana's heart leapt when she recognized her mother's writing. Her fingers trembled as she opened it. Inside was a little brown heart. It was made of bread and had the initials "HB" carved into it. Attached was a letter.

My dearest one, I wish you all the best on your birthday. I am sorry that I can't help you blow out the candles this year. But the heart is a charm I made for your bracelet. Are your clothes getting too small for you? Ask Daddy and Georgie to speak to your aunts about having some new ones made for my big girl. I think about you and your brother all the time. I am well. Are you being a good girl? Will you write me a letter? I hope you and George are keeping up your studies. I am well. I miss you so much, dearest Hanichka. I am kissing you now.

Love, Mother. May 1941. Ravensbruck.

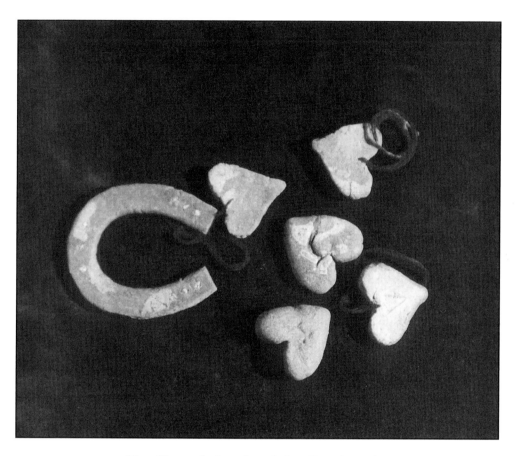

The gifts made from bread that Hana's mother
sent to the family after she was taken away.

Hana closed her eyes and clutched the little brown bread heart. She tried to imagine that her mother was standing beside her.

Jews were ordered to wear yellow cloth stars whenever they went out in public.

That fall brought another blow. One day Father arrived home carrying three squares of cloth. On each was a yellow star of David and in the middle of the star one word: "*Jude*" — Jew.

"Come children," said Father, as he took a pair of scissors from a kitchen drawer. "We need to cut out these stars and pin them on our coats. We must wear them whenever we leave the house."

"Why?" asked Hana. "People already know we are Jews."

"It's what we must do," replied Father. He looked so dejected, sad and tired that Hana and George didn't argue.

From that day on, Hana went outside less often. She would do almost anything to avoid wearing the yellow badge in public. She hated the star. It was so humiliating. It was so embarrassing. Wasn't it enough, the children wondered, that they'd lost their park, their pond, their school and their friends? But now, when they left the house, the star was pinned to their clothing.

One Jewish man in town was not willing to obey. He'd had enough of all the rules and restrictions. So on a late September day in 1941, he left his house feeling a little brazen. He did not cut out the star and pinned the entire cloth to his coat. This tiny act of rebellion was immediately noticed by the Nazi officer in charge in Nové Město na Moravě. He was furious. He declared that Nové Město na Moravě must be made *judenfrei,* free of Jews, immediately.

The very next morning, a big black car driven by a Nazi officer drew up in front of the Bradys' house. Four frightened Jewish men were already huddled inside it. There was a knock on the door. Father opened it. Hana and George hung behind him. The officer barked at Father to come out immediately. Hana and George couldn't believe their ears. They stood there, stunned, terrified and silent. Father hugged the children, implored them to be brave. And then he, too, was gone.

Tokyo,
Spring 2000

FUMIKO WAS ENCHANTED BY HANA'S DRAWINGS. She knew they would help children better imagine what kind of person Hana

Another of Hana's drawings from Theresienstadt.

had been. It would be easier for them to put themselves in her shoes. Fumiko was right.

More than ever, the children who volunteered at the Center focused their attention on Hana. Led by Maiko, some of them formed a group with a mission to let other kids know about what they were learning. They called their club "Small Wings." Once a month, they met to plan their newsletter. Everyone had a role. The older kids wrote articles. The youngest were encouraged to draw pictures. Others wrote poems. With Fumiko's help, they sent their newsletter to schools far and wide, so others could find out about the history of the Holocaust and the search for Hana.

The Small Wings

More than anything, they wanted to know what Hana looked like. They wanted to see the face of this little girl whose story they yearned to know. Fumiko realized that if she could find a photograph of Hana, she would be even more alive to the children as a real human being. Fumiko was determined that the search would continue.

Now that she had the drawings, a sock, the shoe, the sweater, and, of course, Hana's suitcase, Fumiko felt it was time to open the exhibit she had been working towards, "The Holocaust Seen Through Children's Eyes."

Nové Město na Moravě, Winter 1941–1942

NOW THERE WERE ONLY TWO CHILDREN. No parents. George put an arm around his ten-year-old sister and promised to take care of her. Boshka, the housekeeper, tried to distract them with special treats and lighthearted talk. It didn't work. The children were sad and they were very scared.

Hours after their father's arrest there was another knock at the door. Hana's heart pounded. George swallowed hard. Who have they come for now? But when the children opened the door, they found Uncle Ludvik, their beloved Uncle Ludvik. "I've just heard the bad news," he said, hugging Hana with one arm, George with the other. "You are both coming with me. You belong with family, with people who love you."

Uncle Ludvik was a Christian who had married Father's sister. Because he wasn't Jewish, he was not an obvious target for the Nazis. But he was a brave man to take in George and Hana. The Nazis had warned that terrible harm could come to anyone who helped the Jews.

Uncle Ludvik told the children to gather up their most treasured things. Hana took her life-sized doll named Nana whom she had had since she was five. George put together all the family photographs. Each of them filled a suitcase with clothes. Hana chose a large brown suitcase that she had taken before on family trips. She loved the polka-dot lining. When everything was packed, they turned out the light and closed the door behind them.

A younger Hana with George and her doll, Nana, that was almost as big as Hana herself.

That night, her aunt and uncle tucked Hana into a big bed with a feather-filled comforter. "We will care for you until your parents come back, Hana," they promised. "And we'll be just down the hall, if you wake up in the night."

But long after lights out, Hana lay awake, blinking into the unfamiliar darkness. It was a strange bed. And the world — now full of danger — seemed to have turned upside down. What will come

44

next? Hana wondered with fear. Finally, she closed her eyes and fell asleep.

Hana awoke the next morning to urgent barking outside her window. Her heart pounded. What could be wrong? Then she recognized the sounds. It was Sylva, their loyal wolfhound. She had found her way across town to be with Hana and George. At least some friends, Hana thought, stay true. It was a small comfort.

Hana, George and their wolfhound, Sylva.

Aunt Heda and Uncle Ludvik's house was small but comfortable, with a pretty little garden in the back. It was very close to the neighborhood school, and every day George and Hana watched the other children with their book bags, laughing, playing, on their way to their classes. "I want to go too!" Hana stamped her foot in hurt and frustration. But there was nothing anyone could do.

In the months that followed, Uncle Ludvik and Aunt Heda did their best to keep the children busy. George chopped wood for hours on end. Hana read books and played games. She was well liked by her cousins Vera and Jiri. Sometimes she even went to church with them.

Hana and her loving and brave Uncle Ludvik.

Hana and George helping out in the fields.

Later, at Theresienstadt, Hana drew this picture of people working in the fields.

And every day at lunchtime, Hana and George went back to their old home to eat a familiar meal with their housekeeper, Boshka, who pampered them, hugged and kissed them, and reminded them that she had promised their parents that she would keep them healthy by feeding them well.

Every few weeks a letter would arrive from Father, who was imprisoned in the Iglau Nazi prison. George would read only the cheerful part to his sister. George thought Hana was too young to know the whole truth about the harsh conditions in prison and how desperate Father was to be free. She was not too young, though, to be deported by the Nazis.

Nové Město na Moravě, May 1942

ONE DAY, A NOTICE WAS DELIVERED to Aunt Heda and Uncle Ludvik's house. Hana and George Brady were ordered to report to a deportation center at Trebic, fifty kilometers away from Nové Město na Moravě, on May 14, 1942. This was what Uncle Ludvik had feared. He called Hana and George into his study and read them the letter. Then he tried to put the bad news in the best possible light. "You're going on a trip," he told them. "Together! You'll be going to a place where there are lots of other Jews, lots of other children to play with. Maybe there you won't have to wear the star!" George and Hana said very little. They were both unhappy about being uprooted again and leaving their aunt and uncle.

Hana was scared. When Boshka came to help them prepare for this strange trip, Hana peppered her with questions. "Where are our parents? When will we see them again? Where will we end up? What can we take with us?"

JÜDISCHE KULTUSGEMEINDE IN PRAG
ŽIDOVSKÁ NÁBOŽENSKÁ OBEC V PRAZE

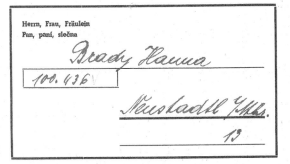

Herrn, Frau, Fräulein
Pan, paní, slečna

Brady Hanna

100.436

Neustadtl 7/1/2.

13

Diese Vorladung ist mit Genehmigung der Zentralstelle für jüdische Auswanderung Prag (Dienststelle des Befehlshabers der Sicherheitspolizei beim Reichsprotektor in Böhmen und Mähren) als Reisegenehmigung anzusehen.	Tato obsílka platí za cestovní povolení na základě schválení Zentralstelle für jüdische Auswanderung Prag (Dienststelle des Befehlshabers der Sicherheitspolizei beim Reichsprotektor in Böhmen und Mähren).
Über Weisung der Zentralstelle für jüdische Auswanderung Prag haben Sie sich	Z nařízení Zentralstelle für jüdische Auswanderung Prag dostavte se

am - dne **30 IV. 1942**

um - v **10** Uhr - hod.

in - do **Trebitsch**

einzufinden.

Jede vorgeladene Person hat mitzubringen	Každá předvolaná osoba přinese s sebou
1. Geburtschein,	1. rodný list,
2. Bürgerlegitimation (Kennkarte oder einen anderen Beleg über die Staatsbürgerschaft),	2. občanskou legitimaci (průkaz totožnosti nebo jiný úřední doklad o státní příslušnosti),
3. diese Vorladung.	3. toto předvolání.
Neben diesen Personaldokumenten hat jede Person sämtliche Lebensmittelkarten mitzubringen.	Kromě těchto osobních dokladů, přinese každá osoba všechny potravinové lístky s sebou.

Um die vorgeschriebene Vorladungsstunde einhalten zu können, werden Sie den	Abyste dodržel(a) hodinu, na kterou jste byl(a) předvolán(a), použijete vlaku, který odjíždí

29.4.42   um - v **18·03** Uhr - hod.

von - z **Neustadtl über Saar**

abgehenden Zug benützen.

Zur Rückreise müssen Sie, den   K návratu musíte nastoupiti do vlaku, který opouští

um - v **16·38** Uhr - hod.

vom Vorladungsort abgehenden Zug benützen.   místo předvolání.

Kinder bis zu 4 Jahren müssen nicht persönlich erscheinen, doch müssen ihre Eltern oder verantwortl. Aufseher, sowohl die Personaldokumente, als auch diese Vorladung und die Lebensmittelkarte vorlegen. Kranke und alte Personen, die nicht persönlich erscheinen können, müssen neben allen Dokumenten ein amtsärztliches Zeugnis vorlegen lassen. Dieses Zeugnis muß eine genaue Diagnose der Krankheit enthalten.	Děti do 4 let se nemusí osobně dostaviti, avšak jejich rodiče nebo jejich zodpov. dozorce musí předložiti jak jejich osobní doklady, tak i toto předvolání a všechny potravinové lístky. Nemocné a staré osoby, které se nemohou osobně dostaviti, dají za sebe předložiti všechny doklady a mimo to vysvědčení úředního lékaře. Toto vysvědčení musí obsahovati přesnou diagnosu nemoci.

JÜDISCHE KULTUSGEMEINDE IN PRAG
ŽIDOVSKÁ NÁBOŽENSKÁ OBEC V PRAZE

This document orders Hana to be deported from her uncle's home on April 30, 1942. In fact, she was sent to Theresienstadt on May 14.

Boshka didn't have any answers. The housekeeper told Hana that she, too, would be leaving Nové Město na Moravě to stay with a brother who lived on a farm.

Hana took out the large brown suitcase with the polka-dot paper lining from under her bed. She packed a sleeping bag that she hoped would give her the smell of home, no matter how far away they were sent. So did George. There was salami and sugar to tuck in amongst the clothes, as well as a few keepsakes.

Uncle Ludvik was heartbroken about sending his young niece and nephew away. He asked a driver to take them to the deportation center; Uncle Ludvik just couldn't face it himself. He and his wife did their best to hide their tears as they said good-bye to Hana and George. They promised to wait for their return to Nové Město na Moravě after the war was over. When the driver rang his bells, and the horses pulled away from the house, no one spoke a word.

A few hours later, the driver dropped Hana and George off in front of a huge warehouse. They joined the lineup near the entrance. When they reached the registration desk, they gave their names to a frowning soldier. He waved them into the dark, airless building.

The floor inside the building was covered with mats. Hana and George found two mats together in a corner and sat down. When they looked around, they realized there were hardly any other children. But there were hundreds of Jewish men and women, waiting to be sent to a place called Theresienstadt. They were all being deported.

For four days and four nights, Hana and George stayed in the warehouse, eating the food from their suitcases, sleeping on the mats. Though some of the adults tried to be kind to the children, Hana and George were not in a mood for company. They had each other and they passed the time reading, talking, napping and thinking of home. It was in this warehouse on May 16, 1942, with a few candies and a stub of a candle, that Hana Brady celebrated her eleventh birthday.

Tokyo,
June 2000

THE EXHIBITION "THE HOLOCAUST SEEN THROUGH CHILDREN'S EYES" drew more visitors, adults and children alike, than Fumiko had dreamed possible. The story of the Holocaust was new to many of the people who came to the Museum. As Fumiko had hoped, its tragedy was made real for them by the objects she had gathered and the story they told.

Though they were interested in the shoe, the can of Zyklon B gas, and the little sweater, it was the suitcase that became a magnet. Children and their parents constantly gathered around it and examined the writing: Hana Brady, May 16, 1931, *Waisenkind* — orphan. They read the poems written by the members of Small Wings. And they admired the drawings Hana had made in Theresienstadt. "Do you know any more about her?" they asked. "What happened to her? What did she look like?" Fumiko decided to re-double her efforts to find a picture of Hana. Somewhere, someone had to be able to help them. Fumiko wrote back to the Terezin Ghetto

Museum. No, came the answer. We already told you. We know nothing about a girl named Hana Brady.

Fumiko just couldn't accept this. She decided to go to Terezin herself.

Deportation Center, May 1942

ON THE MORNING OF THE FOURTH DAY, a loud whistle blew, and a Nazi soldier marched into the warehouse. Hana and George huddled in their corner as he barked out the orders.

"Everyone is to appear at the train tracks in one hour. Each person is allowed one suitcase. Twenty-five kilos. Not a gram more. Form straight lines. No talking. Do as you are told."

The voice was so harsh, so scary. Hana and George quickly got their things together. Adults tried to help them, making sure the children were ready. Poor little ones, they thought. Such a hard journey and alone, with no parents.

Under the threatening eyes of the soldiers, they all left the warehouse in single file and lined up at the tracks. From the brilliant sunlight of the morning, Hana and George stepped into the dark train, carrying their suitcases. More people piled in after them, until it was full. Then the doors slammed shut and the train began to move.

Terezin, July 2000

THERESIENSTADT. The name the Nazis gave the Czech town of Terezin. Fumiko knew that to solve the mystery of Hana's suitcase, she had to get there. But how? The Czech Republic was thousands of miles from Japan and a plane ticket would cost a lot of money that Fumiko didn't have.

But this time luck was on her side. Fumiko was invited to attend a conference on the Holocaust in England. From there, it would only be a short plane trip to Prague, capital of the Czech Republic. From Prague it was just a two-hour drive to Terezin. Fumiko couldn't wait to leave.

On the morning of July 11, 2000, Fumiko got off the bus in the main square of Terezin. At first glance, it looked like an ordinary pretty town. There were wide streets lined with trees and well-kept three-story houses with flowered window boxes. But Fumiko hardly noticed. She had exactly one day to accomplish her mission. That night she would have to go back to Prague. Her plane for Japan was leaving the next morning.

Fumiko hadn't phoned ahead. She had no appointment at the Museum. But directly across from the main square, she saw a long, two-story, pale yellow building. This was the Terezin Ghetto Museum.

Fumiko opened the heavy front door and entered the cool foyer. It was eerily quiet. Where was everybody? She poked her head into a few of the offices off the main entranceway. They were empty. There seemed to be no one in the building.

Fumiko went to modern-day Terezin.

What has happened? Fumiko wondered. Could it be that everyone is out at lunch? No, it's only ten o'clock in the morning. Fumiko went back out into the square and tapped the shoulder of a friendly looking man on a park bench. "Can you help me?" she asked. "I'm looking for someone to speak with in the Museum."

"Oh, you won't find anyone there today, young lady. It's a holiday and all the people who work there are away celebrating," the man replied. "I'm afraid you're out of luck."

Theresienstadt, May 1942

THE TRAIN TRIP WAS QUIET, UNEVENTFUL. People seemed to keep to themselves, lost in their own thoughts and fears about the future. After a few hours, the train came to an abrupt halt. The doors were flung open and the frightened passengers standing nearest to the doors could see the sign reading "Bohusovic Station." Hana squinted in the sunlight as she and George lugged their suitcases off the train. There, at the station, they were instructed to walk the rest of the way to the Theresienstadt fortress.

It was only a few kilometers, but their suitcases were cumbersome and heavy. Should we leave some things here, Hana and George wondered, to lighten our load? No, everything in their suitcases was precious, the only reminders of the life they used to have. George carried one suitcase. The other one they put on a moving cart, pushed by prisoners.

Hana and George approached the entrance to the walled fortress and joined a lineup. Everyone was wearing a yellow star, just like them.

Hana drew this picture of people getting off a train while she was at Theresienstadt.

At the front of the line, a soldier asked people for their name, age and place of birth. Boys and men were being sent in one direction, girls and women in another. "Where are they going?" Hana asked George. More than anything else, she was afraid of being separated from her brother. "Can I stay with you?" she pleaded.

"Be quiet, Hana!" George told his sister. "Don't make a fuss."

When they reached the front of the line, the soldier stared at them. "Where are your parents?" he demanded.

"They are, uh, in another, uh, camp," George stammered. "We hope that here we might be reunited."

The soldier wasn't interested in conversation. He wrote down their names on index cards and searched their suitcases for money and jewelry. Then he slammed the bags shut. "To the left!" he ordered George. "To the right!" he ordered Hana.

"Please can I stay with my brother?" Hana asked.

"Move! Now!" the soldier ordered. What Hana feared most was about to happen. George gave her a quick hug. "Don't worry," he said. "I'll find you as soon as I can." Holding back tears, Hana picked up her suitcase and followed the other girls to *Kinderheim* (children's home) L410, a large barrack for girls that was to be Hana's home for the next two years.

Terezin, July 2000

FUMIKO COULDN'T BELIEVE IT. She was very upset — with herself and with her bad luck. I've come all this way and everyone who might be able to help me is on holiday. How did I manage to pick such a bad time to come to the Terezin Museum? How could I be so stupid? she thought. What do I do now?

As the hot sun beat down on her, a tear of frustration rolled down Fumiko's cheek. She decided to go back inside the Museum to try to collect her thoughts. Maybe she could come up with a different plan.

Sitting on a bench in the foyer, she heard a rustling sound. It appeared to be coming from one of the offices at the end of the hall. Fumiko tiptoed in the direction of the sound. There, in the last office on the right, she found a woman with glasses perched on the end of her nose, sorting through a huge stack of papers.

Startled, the woman almost jumped out of her chair when she saw Fumiko. "Who are you?" she asked. "What are you doing here? The Museum is closed."

"My name is Fumiko Ishioka," she replied. "I have come a long way from Japan to find out about a little girl who was here in Theresienstadt. We have her suitcase in our museum in Tokyo."

"Come back another day," the woman replied politely, "and someone will try and help you."

"But I don't have another day," exclaimed Fumiko. "My plane to Japan leaves tomorrow morning. Please," she pleaded. "Help me find Hana Brady."

The woman removed her glasses. She stared at the young Japanese woman and saw how anxious and determined she was. The Czech woman heaved a sigh. "All right," she said. "I can't promise anything. But I'll try and help you. My name is Ludmila."

Theresienstadt, 1942–43

KINDERHEIM L410 WAS A LARGE, PLAIN BUILDING with about ten dormitory rooms. Twenty girls slept in each room, on burlap mattresses filled with straw in three-tiered bunk beds. Before the war, the town had been home to 5,000 people. The Nazis crammed ten times that number of prisoners into the same space.

There was never enough room, never enough food, never a chance for a private moment. There were too many people, too many bugs and rats, and too many Nazis who patrolled the camp with cruel discipline.

In the beginning, Hana, as a younger child, was not allowed to leave the building. That meant she couldn't see George. He lived in Kinderheim L417, which was just for boys, a few blocks away. Hana missed him terribly, and constantly asked the older girls, who were allowed outside, for news of him. They took Hana under their wing. They felt sorry for her, alone in the world, without her mother and father, away from her brother.

Hana made friends with an older girl in the next bunk. Ella was short, dark and very lively. She had a ready laugh and was happy to spend time with a younger girl who looked up to her and whom she could comfort in difficult times.

The man who gave out tickets for food took a liking to Hana and worried about her health. He knew that Hana was always hungry. He kindly offered to sneak her extra tickets, for another ladle of watery soup, another hunk of black bread. Hana's stomach growled and her mouth watered at the prospect of more food. But each time the offer was made, she politely said no. She'd been warned by Ella and the other older girls that she would be in big trouble with the guards if she was caught breaking a rule.

Torn from their families, crammed into small spaces, with barely enough to eat, the girls set about trying to make the best of a very bad situation. The ones over fifteen worked in the garden, where fruits, vegetables and flowers were grown for the Nazi soldiers. Once in a while, Mr. Schwartzbart, who ran the garden, allowed Hana to come out with the working group and enjoy the fresh air and sun. Hana loved the chance to work in the garden with the older girls. And there was an added bonus. A green bean here, and a strawberry there, always managed to find its way into a hungry girl's mouth.

But for the most part, Hana had to stay with girls her own age or younger, and obey the supervisor assigned to her room. Every day, they dusted, cleaned and swept under the bunks. Dishes, as well as faces, were washed under a pump.

And every day there were secret classes held in the attic of Kinderheim L410.

In music classes, the girls learned new songs. They sang softly so they wouldn't be heard by the guards. At the end of each class, one child was chosen to sing a favorite song from home. When it was Hana's turn, she always sang a song called "Stonozka," the centipede song.

Her life is not a piece of cake.
Imagine how she suffers when
She walks until her tootsies ache.
She's got good reason to complain.
So when I want to cry the blues
I just recall the centipede.
Consider walking in her shoes
And then my life seems sweet indeed.

There were sewing classes, too. Hana had never sewn a stitch in her life, and she had a hard time with the needle. The teacher often had to ask Hana to stop giggling when she made a silly mistake. Nonetheless she managed to finish a blue blouse of which she was very proud.

But Hana's favorite class was her art class. Painting and drawing supplies were hard to come by. Some people had smuggled them into the ghetto in suitcases. Paper had been stolen, sometimes at great risk, from the Nazi storerooms. Plain wrapping paper was used when nothing else could be

Hana's drawing of people having a picnic under an umbrella, beside a river.

found. One way or another, in the early days, there were always crayons and colored pencils.

The art teacher, Friedl Dicker-Brandeis, had been a famous painter and was now a fellow prisoner at Theresienstadt. Friedl taught her students about serious things like perspective and texture. And sometimes the girls drew pictures of serious subjects: the ghetto walls, people waiting in line for food, inmates being beaten by Nazi soldiers.

But, more than anything, Friedl wanted her classes to help the children forget their brutal surroundings, at least for a while. "Think of space," she told Hana and the others. "Think of freedom. Let your imagination run wild. Tell me what is in your hearts. Put it down on paper."

Sometimes, she would take them to the roof of the building, so they could be closer to the sky. From there, they could look beyond the walls of the camp and see the surrounding mountains in the distance. The girls could dream of birds and butterflies, of ponds and swings. And, using their crayons and pencils, they could bring them to life.

When classes were over and all the chores were done, they played a board game called *Smelina*, which had been invented right there in the ghetto. It was based on Monopoly, created for the children by an engineer named Oswald Pock who had been deported to Terezin. The players would land on properties like *Entwesung*, the de-lousing station where clothes were disinfected, and the guards' barracks. Instead of building a hotel, players built a *kumbal*, an attic hideaway above the barracks. For money, players used the ghetto paper bills called ghetto *kronen*.

But no matter what the distractions, Hana always ended up feeling hungry and lonely. She missed George terribly. Then one day there was an announcement that the ghetto rules were changing. The girls were allowed to go out once a week for two hours.

Hana immediately raced across the square to the Boys'

House. "George, George Brady!" she called. "Where is my brother? Have you seen my brother?" She ran from room to room, asking every boy she came across. So anxious was Hana to find her brother that she even opened the door to a bathroom. And there was George, working away at his new job as a plumber. What a joyous reunion it was! George threw down his tools and Hana rushed into his arms. They laughed. They cried. Questions tumbled from their mouths. "Are you well? Have you heard anything about Mother and Father? Are you getting enough to eat?" From then on, they took advantage of every opportunity to be together.

George took his responsibility as a big brother seriously. He felt it was his job to protect Hana and to make sure she didn't get into trouble. He wanted to keep her as happy and healthy as possible until they could be with their parents again.

And Hana was equally devoted to George. In Terezin, where there was never enough to eat, residents received a small *buchta,* a plain doughnut, once a week. Hana never ate hers. She brought it to George so he could be strong and stay sweet.

In Theresienstadt, it seemed to Hana that more people arrived every day. Men, women and children came from all over Czechoslovakia at first, and then from other European countries. Every time a new group of people got off the trains, Hana would look for familiar faces. And sometimes, when she was feeling strong, she would approach strangers and ask, "Do you know my mother and father? Have you been to a place called Ravensbruck? My mother is there! Do you have any news of Karel and Marketa Brady?" The answer was always the same, but delivered with kindness and a barely concealed pity. "No dear, we don't know your mother and father. But if we hear anything — anything at all — we will find you and tell you."

Then one day, a familiar face did appear — an old friend of her parents who had no children of her own. At first, Hana was thrilled to see her. Anything that reminded Hana of home, that brought her a tiny step closer to her mother and father, was a comfort. But suddenly it seemed that wherever Hana went, the woman was waiting for her. Every time Hana turned a corner, she was there. She pinched Hana's cheek, gave her kisses. And then one day, she went too far.

"Come here, little one," she said, holding her hand out. "Remember all our good times together. Don't be shy. Don't be lonely. You can come and see me every day. You can call me 'mother.'"

"I have a mother," Hana spat out. "Go away! Leave me alone." Hana refused to see the woman again. She missed her own mother. No one could take her place.

Terezin, July 2000

AT THE TEREZIN GHETTO MUSEUM, Ludmila sat down behind her desk and stared at the young Japanese woman perched on the edge of the seat across from her. Fumiko's strong determination was written all over her face. Ludmila liked Fumiko and wanted to help her find out more about this girl, this Hana Brady.

She pulled a big book off the shelves. Inside were the names of the almost 90,000 men, women and children who had been imprisoned at Theresienstadt and transported to the east. They turned to the B's: Brachova, Hermina. Brachova, Zusana. Brada, Tomas. Bradacova, Marta. Bradleova, Zdenka.

"Here she is," cried Ludmila. And there she was: Hana Brady, May 16, 1931. "How can I find out more about her?" Fumiko asked.

"I wish I knew," Ludmila replied.

"But look," said Fumiko, pointing to another line in the book. There was another Brady, listed right over Hana. "Could this be her family?" Fumiko wondered aloud. Ludmila looked at the birth dates. Three years apart. "Yes," she said, "chances are very good that this was a brother. The Nazis listed families together."

There was something else that Fumiko noticed. Beside Hana's name was a check mark. In fact, there was a check mark beside every name on the page — except one. Beside the other Brady, George Brady, there was nothing. What did this mean?

581	Wolfenstein Helene	Haushalt	15. 6. 1890	Gr. Meseritsch Oberstadt 350	100716
582	Wolfenstein Walter	Arbeiter	19.10. 1913	Gr. Meseritsch Oberstadt 350	100719
583	Wolfenstein Sidonie	Schneiderin	10. 1. 1911	Gr. Meseritsch Oberstadt 350	100718
584	Schück Ing. Friedrich	Masch.Ing.	23. 6. 1891	Unter Bobrau 81 Dolní Bobrové	100646
585	Drechsler Simon	Kaufmann	3. 8. 1885	Gr. Meseritsch Dalimilg.35	100483
586	Schnabel Rudolfine	Haushalt	20. 3. 1877	Unter Bobrau 81	100642
587	Schück Dr. Ottokar	Arzt	4.11. 1894	Unter Bobrau 81	100648
588	Schück Edith	Haushalt	17. 5. 1907	Unter Bobrau 81	100647
589	Schück Ingmar	Schülerin	30. 3. 1933	Unter Bobrau 81	100645
590	Schück Zdenko	Schüler	31. 7. 1938	Unter Bobrau 81	100650
591	Fein Anna	Private	9. 6. 1890	Neustadtl 1.M.123 Nové Město Moravé	100491
592	Lauer Irma	Hausgehilfin	31. 8. 1932	Teltsch Radekgl.181 dzt.Trebitsch Iglauer Tor 1 Jelí	100117
593	Thierfeld Emma	Haushalt	13. 3. 1887	Stadt Saar 65	100636
594	Schwartz Irene T.	Fotografin	3.12. 1915	Stadt Saar 65 Měšto Žďár	100654
595	Thierfeld Paul	Arbeiter	16. 3. 1936	Stadt Saar 65	100633
596	Brady Georg	Schüler	9. 2. 1928	Neustadtl 1.M.13	100435
597	Brady Hana	Schülerin	16. 5. 1931	Neustadtl 1.M.13	100436
598	Jillisch Anna	Haushalt	27. 1. 1901	Bochesetz 28 Březejc	100714
599	Blum Irene	Haushalt	15.10. 1891	Gr. Meseritsch Dalimilg.22	100433
600	Buchsbaum Elsa	Haushalt	13.13. 1892	Gr. Meseritsch Dalimilg.22	100418

From this list Fumiko learns that Hana had a brother.

Theresienstadt, 1943–44

As THE DAYS AND MONTHS PASSED, Theresienstadt became more crowded and cramped. New trainloads of people arrived all the time. This meant that there was less food for everyone and people became weak and sick. The oldest and youngest people were most at risk.

One day, after she had been in the ghetto for a year, Hana received an urgent message from her brother: Meet me at the Boys' House at six in the evening. I have a wonderful surprise for you.

George couldn't wait to share the good news. "Grandmother is here! She arrived last night!"

The children were overjoyed at the thought of seeing their grandmother. They were also worried. George and Hana's grandmother had been a refined woman who lived a cultured, comfortable life in the capital city of Prague. It was this generous grandmother who had given them their scooters. When they visited her in the big city, she always gave

The now-renovated girls' barracks in Theresienstadt, where Hana lived.

them bananas and oranges. But in recent years, she had been quite ill. How would she manage in this awful place? Not well, it turned out.

The children found her in an overcrowded attic, with only straw to sleep on, one of many old, sick people. It was the middle of July and the attic was boiling hot. They were horrified by what they saw. Their gentle, elegant grandmother looked terrible. Her beautiful white hair, always so perfectly combed in the past, was a mess. Her clothes were torn and soiled. "I've brought you one of my paintings," Hana exclaimed, thinking it might put a smile on the old woman's face. But her grandmother could barely turn her head. Instead Hana folded the coarse paper and made her painting into a fan. "Rest," she told her grandmother as she tried to create a cooling breeze. Hana felt proud to be in charge of trying to help her grandmother feel better.

Hana soon learned that old people in Theresienstadt were given the smallest and worst rations. The food her grandmother got just wasn't enough and was often crawling with bugs. And there was no medicine. The children visited as often as they could and tried to cheer her up, bringing crafts they'd made and singing songs they'd learned. "This bad time will all be over soon," George told her. "Mother and Father are counting on us all to stay strong," Hana said.

But in three months time, their grandmother was dead. Beyond Hana and George, few people took much notice. Death was all around them. In fact, so many people were dying so fast, the cemetery was full. Clinging to each other, Hana and George tried to remember the happy times with their grandmother, and cried together.

As more people poured into Terezin, thousands more poured out. They were crammed into boxcars and sent eastward to an unknown fate. Rumors about the transports spread inside the walls of Theresienstadt. Some tried to convince themselves and others that a better life awaited the people who were sent away on the trains. But as time went on, stories of death camps, brutality and mass murder circulated widely. When people spoke of these things, Hana covered her ears.

Every few weeks, the dreaded lists would be posted in each building. People whose names were on them had to report to an assembly hall close to the railway station within two days.

Lists. Everywhere there were lists. The Nazis were systematic record keepers and they wanted all their prisoners to know it. Through the constant counting and listing of people, the Nazis reminded the inmates who was in charge. Everyone knew that being counted, being noticed, could mean a transport and another separation from family and friends.

One morning, as Hana was doing her chores, everyone in the camp was ordered to stop what they were doing and assemble on a huge field outside the town. Everyone — old and young. They were marched out by Nazi guards carrying machine guns, and ordered to stand there with no food, no water, and a sense that something terrible was about to happen. Hana and the other girls didn't even dare to whisper among themselves.

Hana couldn't bear the thought that she might be separated from George. Or from the girls in Kinderheim L410, who had become almost like sisters. Wasn't it enough that her parents had been taken away from her? Ella stood beside her and tried to cheer her up with smiles and winks.

But after four hours of standing, Hana could no longer contain her despair. She began to cry.

Ella slipped her a tiny piece of bread she had hidden in her coat. "Eat this, Hana," she quietly implored. "You will feel better." But Hana's tears kept coming. The big girl then turned to her. "Listen carefully to me," she whispered. "You are unhappy and scared. That's just how the Nazis want to see us, all of us. You can't give them the satisfaction, Hana. You can't give them what they want. We are stronger and better than that. You must dry up those tears, Hana, and put on a brave face." Miraculously, Hana did.

The Nazi commander began shouting out names. Everyone had to be accounted for. Finally, after eight hours of standing in a bitter wind, everyone was ordered to march back to the barracks.

It was September, 1944. When the Nazis began to realize that they were losing the war they announced that more people would be leaving Theresienstadt. The transports were sped up. Now a new list of names went up every day.

Each morning, her heart pounding, Hana ran down to the main entrance of the building where the list was posted. And one day there it was — the name she dreaded finding — George Brady. Hana's knees buckled. She sat down on the ground and cried. George, her beloved brother, her protector, was being sent away to the east. That wiry boy, now a young man, was told to report to the trains along with 2,000 other able-bodied men.

At their last meeting, on the dirt path between the Boys' House and Kinderheim L410, George asked Hana to listen carefully. "I leave tomorrow," he said. "Now, more than ever, you must eat as much as you can. You must breathe fresh air at every opportunity. You must take care of your health. Be strong. Here is my last ration. Eat every last crumb."

George gave Hana a huge bear hug and gently pushed the hair out of her eyes. "I promised Mother and Father that I would take care of you and bring you home safely so that we can all be together as a family again. I don't want to break that promise." Then the curfew whistle screamed and George was gone.

Hana became despondent. She couldn't bear the separation from her brother. First her parents, and now George. She felt so terribly alone in the world. Sometimes, when the other girls tried to cheer her up, Hana turned her face away or even snapped at them, "Can't you just leave me alone?"

Only gentle Ella could convince her to eat her meager rations. "Remember what your brother told you. You need to take care of yourself and stay strong — for him."

Four weeks later, Hana learned that she, too, was going east. A reunion! "I'll see George again," she told everyone. "He's waiting for me."

She sought out Ella. "Can you help me?" she asked. "I want to look nice when I see my brother. I want to show him how well I've taken care of myself." Despite her own fears, Ella wanted to nourish the hopes of her young friend. She smiled at Hana and set to work. She got water at the pump and used her last little square of soap to wash Hana's face and to clean her knotted, dirty hair. With a piece of rag she tied Hana's hair into a ponytail. She pinched Hana's cheeks to bring up a little red. Ella stood back and looked at the results of her efforts. Hana's face shone with hope. "Thank you Ella," Hana said, hugging the bigger girl. "I don't know what I would do without you." For the first time since George had been sent away, she looked happy.

That night, Hana packed her suitcase. There wasn't much to put into it: a few pieces of pretty worn out clothing, one of her favorite drawings from Friedl's art class, a book of stories that Ella had given her. When she was done, Hana got into her bunk and slept her last night in Theresienstadt.

The next morning, she and many of the other girls from Kinderheim L410 were marched out to the railroad track. Nazi guards barked orders and their dogs bared their teeth and growled. No one stepped out of line.

"Where do you think we are going?" Hana whispered to Ella. No one really knew. The girls boarded the darkened rail car one by one, until there was not an inch of room left in the train. The air turned sour. And the wheels began to turn.

The train chugged on for a day and a night. There was no food. There was no water. There was no toilet. The girls had no idea how long the journey would be. Their throats were parched, their bones ached, their stomachs twitched with hunger.

They tried to comfort each other, singing songs of home. "Lean on me," Ella said softly, "and listen, Hana."

So when I want to cry the blues
I just recall the centipede.
Consider walking in her shoes
And then my life seems sweet indeed.

The girls held hands. They closed their eyes and tried to imagine being somewhere else. Each girl imagined something different. When Hana closed her eyes, she saw the strong, smiling face of her brother.

And then suddenly, in the middle of the night on October 23, 1944, the wheels of the train ground to a screeching halt. The doors were opened. The girls were ordered out of the boxcar. This was Auschwitz.

An angry guard ordered them to stand straight and silent on the platform. He held tight the leash of a large dog straining to pounce. The guard looked the group up and down quickly. He cracked his whip in the direction of one girl who had always been embarrassed by how tall she was. "You," he said, "over there, to the right!" He cracked his whip one more time at another of the older girls. "You, there too." Then he called over to a group of young soldiers who stood at the edge of the platform. "Take them, now!" he ordered, pointing to Hana and the rest of her group. Huge searchlights almost blinded the girls. "Leave your suitcases on the platform," the soldiers commanded.

Through a wrought iron gate and under the watchful eyes of the surly dogs and uniformed men, Hana and her old roommates were marched off. Hana held on tight to Ella's hand. They passed huge barracks, saw the skeleton-like faces of prisoners in their striped uniforms peeking out the doors. They were ordered to enter a large building. The door closed behind them with a frightening bang.

Terezin, July 2000

"WHAT DOES THE CHECK MARK MEAN?" asked Fumiko, as she looked at the page listing Hana Brady and George Brady.

Ludmila hesitated and then spoke carefully. "The check mark means that the person didn't survive."

Fumiko lowered her eyes to the paper again. Hana's name had a check mark beside it. Like almost all the 15,000 children who passed through Theresienstadt, Hana had died at Auschwitz.

Fumiko bowed her head and closed her eyes. She had already guessed the awful truth. But hearing it spoken, seeing it on paper was still a blow. Fumiko sat silently for a few minutes, trying to take it all in.

And then she gathered herself together and looked up. Hana's story was not over. Now, more than ever, Fumiko wanted to know everything about her — for herself, for the children waiting for her back in Japan, and for Hana's memory. She was absolutely determined that this life, ended so unjustly, at such a young age, would not be forgotten. It had become her mission to make sure of this. The quest was not over.

"There is no check mark beside George's name," Fumiko said. "Is there any way," she stammered, "that we can find out about him? What happened to him? Where did he go? Is he still alive?" If she could only find him, he might help her discover more about Hana. Fumiko began to tremble with excitement.

Ludmila looked sadly across the desk at Fumiko. She could see how badly Fumiko wanted to know. "I have no idea what happened to him," she said softly. "The war was such a long time ago, you know. He could have gone anywhere in the world. He could even have changed his name. Or he could have died, long after the war."

"Please," Fumiko pleaded, "you have to help me find him."

The woman sighed and turned back to the bookshelves crammed with bound volumes of names on lists. "We can keep looking for clues in here," she said. For an hour, Fumiko and Ludmila sorted through books filled with names, looking for another mention of George Brady. And finally, they found one.

He was on the list of inmates of Kinderheim L417, the Boys' House at Theresienstadt. The names were clumped in groups of six, since two boys shared each mattress in the three-tiered bunks. When Ludmila checked the names listed with George Brady, she looked up at Fumiko with a start.

"Kurt Kotouc," she said. "Kurt Kotouc," she repeated. "I know that name. He's alive. I think George Brady's bunkmate used to live in Prague, but I have no idea where. If we can locate him, maybe he can tell you what happened to Hana's brother. Unfortunately, there's nothing more I can do for you here. Try the Jewish Museum in Prague. Maybe someone there can help."

Fumiko thanked Ludmila over and over again for all she had done. She hugged her and promised to let her know about the results of her sleuthing. Ludmila wished Fumiko luck. Then Fumiko picked up her briefcase and ran out of the office into the town square. The bus for Prague was due at any moment.

Prague, July 2000

FUMIKO HAD ONLY A FEW HOURS OF DAYTIME remaining before her plane left for Japan early the next morning. As soon as she got off the bus in Prague, she hailed a taxi. "The Jewish Museum, please," she said, trying to catch her breath.

She arrived at the Prague Jewish Museum just before closing time. The guard told her to come back the next day. "But I can't," pleaded Fumiko. "I have to go back to Japan tomorrow morning. I'm here to see Michaela Hajek. She helped me find some very important drawings." When nothing else seemed to convince the guard, Fumiko bent the truth a little. "She's expecting me," Fumiko told the man confidently. And he let her in.

This time, luck was on Fumiko's side. The woman was in her office and remembered the story of Hana. She listened carefully as Fumiko explained what she had found out.

"I have heard of Kurt Kotouc," Michaela said quietly. Fumiko could barely believe it. "I will try and help you find him," Michaela promised. She understood that Fumiko had no time to lose.

Fumiko sat quietly as Michaela made phone call after phone call. Each person Michaela spoke to gave her another number to try and wished her well in the search. Finally she reached an office where Mr. Kotouc worked as an art historian. She handed the phone to Fumiko who tried to explain what she was looking for. The secretary wanted to help, but told her Mr. Kotouc was leaving on an overseas trip that evening. "I'm sorry," she said to Fumiko, "a meeting will be impossible." No, he didn't even have time for a phone call.

Michaela watched as Fumiko's face fell. She got back on the phone herself and pleaded with the secretary. "You have no idea how desperate this young woman is. She has to go back to Japan in the morning. This is her only chance." The secretary finally relented.

Two hours later, the sky was dark and the Museum was officially closed. All the staff had gone home. But one office was still brightly lit. There, Fumiko and Michaela awaited the arrival of Mr. Kotouc.

Finally he came. The heavyset man with bright eyes had much to tell. "I only have half an hour," he said, "before I leave for the airport. Of course, I remember George Brady. We shared a bunk in Theresienstadt and much more. You never forget the connections you make with people in a place like Theresienstadt. Not only that," he said, "we are still friends. He lives in Toronto, Canada."

Mr. Kotouc pulled out a small leather book. "Here's what you're looking for," he said with a smile.

He wrote down George Brady's address and gave it to Fumiko. "Oh, Mr. Kotouc, I can't thank you enough," Fumiko said.

"Good luck," he told Fumiko. "I'm so happy that children in Japan want to understand the lessons of the Holocaust." And then Mr. Kotouc practically flew out of the office, baggage in hand.

Fumiko beamed from ear to ear. All her persistence had paid off. She told Michaela how grateful she was for her help.

The next morning Fumiko settled in her seat for the long flight to Japan. She was still tingling with excitement. She tried to recall all the news she had for the children at the Center. When she thought about Hana having a big brother, Fumiko couldn't help picturing her own little sister, three years younger. Fumiko had always been her protector and she tried to imagine what she would do if her little sister were in danger. The very thought made her shudder. She looked out the window as the story repeated itself over and over in her mind. After an hour, she fell into a deep sleep, the first one she'd had in a long time.

Tokyo, August 2000

BACK IN TOKYO, Fumiko called a special meeting of Small Wings. She shared every detail of her adventure with the members. The sad news came first. With the children around her in a circle, Fumiko told them, in a quiet voice, what they had already imagined. Hana had died at Auschwitz.

"But I have a wonderful surprise," Fumiko said. The faces of the children brightened. "Hana had a brother named George — and he survived!"

The questions started flying at once. "Where is he?" asked Maiko. "How old is he?" one boy wanted to know. "Does he know that we have Hana's suitcase?" asked Akira. Fumiko told them everything she knew. And she said she would work late that very night so that she could write George a letter.

"Can we send something with it?" asked Maiko. The older kids scattered to quiet spots around the Center to compose poems. "What can I do?" Akira asked Maiko.

"Draw a picture of Hana," she replied.

"But I don't know what she looks like," he said.

"Just draw her as you imagine her," Maiko said. And Akira did.

Fumiko wrote her own letter very carefully. She knew that receiving it would come as a shock to George. She knew that some Holocaust survivors refused to ever speak about their experiences. She worried that his memories might be so bitter and painful that he wouldn't want to hear anything about Hana's suitcase and the Holocaust Center in Japan.

Fumiko had copies made of Hana's drawings and packaged them carefully, along with the children's writings and artwork. Then she took the parcel down to the post office, crossed her fingers, and sent it off to Canada.

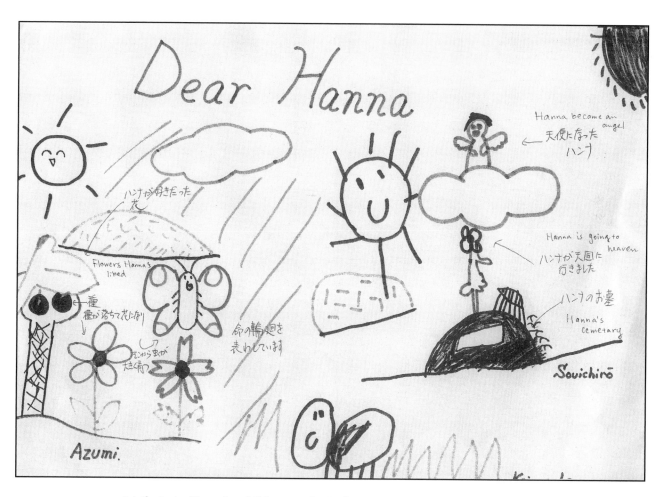

A tribute to Hana by children at the Holocaust Center. They used the German spelling of Hana's name because it was spelled that way on the suitcase.

Toronto, Canada
August 2000

IT WAS A WARM AND SUNNY AUGUST AFTERNOON. Seventy-two-year-old George Brady had come home from work early and had planned to spend a quiet afternoon in the empty house, clearing up some bills. He was sitting at his dining room table when he heard the footsteps of the mailman, the whoosh of envelopes being shoved through the slot, and the thunk of them landing on the floor. I'll get them later, he thought. Then the doorbell rang.

When he opened the door, the mailman was standing there. "This wouldn't fit through," he said, handing a package to George. The package was postmarked Japan. What could this be? George wondered. He didn't know anyone in Japan.

When he opened the package and began to read the letter, George's heart began to pound. He closed his eyes. He opened them, blinking hard, making sure that what he was reading was real. Was this a daytime dream he was having?

George Brady today.

The loss of his sister Hana was George's most private and deepest sorrow. He had lived with it for over half a century and had never been able to get over the feeling that he should have been able to protect his little sister.

Now, somehow, halfway around the world, her story was being told and her life was being honored. George was stunned. He sat down and let his mind wander back fifty-five years.

When Auschwitz was liberated in January 1945, George Brady was seventeen years old. He had survived the horrors of the camp by starting out young and strong, by good luck, and by using the trade he had learned at Theresienstadt — plumbing. When he was freed, he was very weak and painfully thin. But George was determined to make his way back to Nové Město na Moravě — to his parents and his little sister Hana. He desperately wanted his family to be together again.

By foot, by train and by hitchhiking, George made it back to the home he loved in May 1945. He went straight for Uncle Ludvik and Aunt Heda's house. It was the last place where he had known family, love and safety. When they opened the door and found their nephew standing there, aunt and uncle fell on him — hugging, kissing, touching, crying — barely able to believe that George was alive.

But the unbridled happiness of the reunion was short-lived. "Where are Mother and Father?" George asked. Ludvik and Heda were forced to tell him the terrible truth. Marketa had been sent from Ravensbruck to Auschwitz and murdered there in 1942. Karel was killed there the same year. "And Hana?" George whispered. All his aunt and uncle knew was that she had been sent to Auschwitz.

For months, George nursed the faint hope that somehow, somewhere, Hana would appear. He searched for her in every young girl's face he saw, in every ponytail that swished by, in every jaunty step of a healthy child on the street. One day, George encountered a teenaged girl on the main street in Prague. She stopped in front of him.

"George?" she asked. "Are you not George Brady, Hana's

brother? My name is Marta. I knew Hana. All of us older girls at Theresienstadt loved her." George searched Marta's eyes for information, for hope. She realized that George didn't yet know the final truth about his sister. "George," she told him quietly, plainly, taking hold of his hands. "Hana was sent to be killed in the gas chamber at Auschwitz, the same day she arrived there. I'm sorry, George. Hana is dead." George's knees turned to jelly and the world went black.

〒160-0015 東京都新宿区大京町28-105
TEL:03-5363-4808 FAX:03-5363-4809
28-105 Daikyo-cho,Shinjuku-ku Tokyo,160-0015 JAPAN
TEL:+81-3-5363-4808 FAX:+81-3-5363-4809
E-mail:Holocaust@Tokyo.email.ne.jp
Homepage:http://www.ne.jp/asahi/holocaust/tokyo

ホロコースト教育資料センター
Tokyo Holocaust Education Resource Center

~*For Children, Builders of Peace*

Mr. George Brady
23 Blyth Hill Road
Toronto 12, M4N 3L5
CANADA

August 22, 2000

Dear Mr. Brady,

We take a liberty of addressing and telling you about our activities in Japan. My name is Fumiko Ishioka and I am Director of Tokyo Holocaust Education Resource Center. In July this year I met with Mr. Kurt Jiri Kotouc in Prague and I got your address from him. The reason why I am writing to you is because we are now exhibiting your sister, Hanna Brady's suitcase at our Center. Please forgive me if my letter hurts you reminding you of your past difficult experiences. But I would very much appreciate it if you could kindly spare some time to read this letter.

Please let me start with a little explanation on what we do in Japan. Tokyo Holocaust Education Resource Center, established in October 1998, is a non-profit, educational organization that aims at further promoting understanding of the history of the Holocaust especially among young children in this country. Children here do not have a chance to learn about the Holocaust, but we believe it is our responsibility too to let our next generation learn the lessons of the Holocaust so that such a tragedy would never be repeated again anywhere in the world. As well as learning the truth of the Holocaust, it is also very important for children, we believe, to think about what they can do to fight against racism and intolerance and to create peace by their own hands.

Besides welcoming children at our Center for exhibition and study programs, this year we organized a pair of traveling exhibition, "The Holocaust Seen Through Children's Eyes" in order to reach more children living far from our Center. For this project, we borrowed some children's memorial items from individuals and museums in Europe, one of which is Hanna Brady's suitcase from the museum of Auschwitz. Many children are now visiting our Center to see this suitcase to learn about the Holocaust. In June, furthermore, we held the Children's Forum on the Holocaust 2000, where our Center's children's group "Small Wings" did a little opening performance on Hanna's suitcase. "Small Wings" is a group of children, aged from 8 to 18, who write newsletters and make videos to let their friends know about the Holocaust and share what they learn from it. At the Forum they decided to use Hanna's suitcase to do an introduction for their friends who have never heard of the Holocaust. It successfully helped participants of the Forum focus on one little life, among one and a half million, lost during the Holocaust, and think about importance of remembering this history.

When I received the suitcase from the museum of Auschwitz, all the information I had were things written on the suitcase, her name and her birthday, and from the Terezin memorial book I got the date when she was deported to Auschwitz. I could also find 4 of her drawings from Terezin. But that was all. Hoping to get more information on Hanna, I went to Terezin in July, when I found your name on the list I got from the ghetto museum and heard that you survived. I was then so lucky to find Mr. Kotouc in Prague and met with him, from whom I heard you now live in Toronto. Those children of "Small Wings" were all so excited to know Hanna had a brother and he survived.

I was wondering if you would kindly be able to tell us about you and Hanna's story, the time you spent with Hanna before sent to the camp, things that you talked with her, you and her dreams, and anything that would help children here feel close to you and Hanna to understand what prejudice, intolerance and hatred did to young Jewish children. If possible, I would be grateful if you could lent us any kind of memorial items such as your family's photo, and so on. It will greatly help us further promote our goal to give every child in Japan a chance to learn about the Holocaust.

Thank you very much for your time. I would very much appreciate your kind understanding for our activities.

I look forward to hearing from you.

With kindest regards,

Fumiko Ishioka
Director
Tokyo Holocaust Education Resource Center

Fumiko's letter to George.

96

Toronto, August 2000

IN THE MORE THAN HALF A CENTURY since George learned the terrible fates of his parents and sister, much had happened. At seventeen, George had left Nové Město na Moravě. He moved from city to city in Europe, carrying his only treasured possession — the box of family photographs that Uncle Ludvik and Aunt Heda had hidden for him. Then, in early 1951, he moved to Toronto and set up a plumbing business with another Holocaust survivor. It was very successful. George married, became the father of three sons and, much later, of a daughter.

George was proud that — despite his suffering during the Holocaust and the fact that his mother, father and sister had been murdered by the Nazis — he had moved on with his life. He was a successful businessman, a proud father. He thought of himself as a healthy person who, for the most part, put his wartime experiences behind him. But whatever he accomplished, whatever joy he felt, it was always tinged with the memory of his beautiful little sister and the horror of her fate.

And now, here he was, with a letter from halfway around the world, telling him how his sister's suitcase was helping a new generation of Japanese children learn about the Holocaust. The letter from Fumiko also asked, very gently, for his help.

Please forgive me, if my letter hurts you by reminding you of your difficult experiences. But I would very much appreciate if you would kindly be able to tell us about your and Hana's story. We would like to know about the time you spent with Hana before you were sent to the camp, the things that you talked with her about, your and her dreams. We are interested in anything that would help children here in Japan feel close to you and Hana. We want to understand what prejudice, intolerance, and hatred did to young Jewish children.

If possible, I would also be grateful if you could lend us any family photos. I know that most Holocaust survivors lost their family photographs, along with their families. But if you do have any pictures, it would greatly help us with our goal to give every child in Japan a chance to learn about the Holocaust. We at the Tokyo Holocaust Center and the children of Small Wings are all so excited to know that Hana had a brother and that he survived.

It was signed "Fumiko Ishioka."

George could hardly believe it. Such amazing connections and strange coincidences had brought three worlds together: the world of children in Japan, George in Canada, and the lost world of a Jewish girl from Czechoslovakia who died so long ago. George wiped the tears from his cheek and then smiled to himself. Hana's young face was so clear to him. He could almost hear her laugh, and feel her soft hand in his. George went to the large wooden dresser and pulled out a photograph album. He wanted to get in touch with Fumiko Ishioka as soon as possible.

Tokyo, September 2000

EVER SINCE SHE HAD SENT THE LETTER TO TORONTO, Fumiko had been a bundle of nerves. Would George Brady write back? Will he help us to know Hana? Even the letter carrier who delivered the mail to the Center knew how anxious Fumiko was. "Anything from Canada today?" she would ask the minute she saw him walking up the path to the front door. He hated to see her disappointment when, day after day, the answer was no.

Then on the last day of September, Fumiko was in the middle of welcoming forty guests at the Center. They were teachers and students who had come to learn about the Holocaust and to see the suitcase. Out of the corner of her eye, through a window, she saw the letter carrier walking very quickly toward the building with a huge smile on his face. Fumiko excused herself and ran to meet him. "Here it is," he said, beaming. And he handed her a thick envelope from Toronto.

"Oh thank you," Fumiko cried. "Thank you for making my day!"

She took the letter to her office and opened it. As she unfolded the pages, photos spilled out. Four photographs of Hana, her blonde hair shining around her smiling face.

Hana

Fumiko screamed. She couldn't help it. Some of the visiting teachers and students rushed to her office door. "What's wrong? What's the matter?" they asked.

"Nothing is wrong," she told them, stumbling over her words. "I'm just so happy, so excited. Here, look, this is a picture of Hana. This is the beautiful little girl whose story we have worked so hard to find."

Along with the photographs, there was a long letter from George. In it, Fumiko learned about Hana's happy early days in Nové Město na Moravě, about her family, and how she loved to ski and skate. It was comforting to know that Hana had had a good life before the war ruined everything.

And Fumiko learned about George, too. As she read about his life in Canada, his children and his grandchildren, Fumiko was bursting with happiness. She began to cry. He survived, she repeated over and over to herself. He survived. More than that, he has a beautiful family. She couldn't wait to tell the children of Small Wings.

Tokyo, March 2001

"CALM DOWN," FUMIKO SAID WITH A SMILE. "They'll be here soon, I promise."

But nothing she said could tame the excitement of the children that morning. They buzzed around the Center, checked their poems, straightened their clothes for the umpteenth time, told silly jokes just to make the time move faster. Even Maiko, whose job it was to calm everyone else down, was jumpy.

Then, finally, the waiting was over. George Brady had arrived. And he had brought with him his seventeen-year-old daughter, Lara Hana.

Now the children became very quiet. At the Center's front entrance, they crowded around George. They bowed to him, as is the custom in Japan. George bowed back. Akira presented George with a beautiful multi-colored origami garland. All the children jostled gently for the chance to be nearest to him. After so many months of hearing about George from Fumiko, they were thrilled to finally meet him in person.

*Fumiko holds a picture of the suitcase as George Brady talks
to children during his trip to Japan and the Holocaust Center.*

Fumiko took George's arm. "Come with us, now, and see your sister's suitcase." They walked to the display area.

And there, surrounded by the children, with Fumiko holding one of his hands and his daughter, Lara, holding the other, George saw the suitcase.

Suddenly, an almost unbearable sadness came over him. Here was the suitcase. There was her name written right on it. Hana Brady. His beautiful, strong, mischievous, generous, fun-loving sister. She had died so young and in such a terrible way. George lowered his head and let the tears flow freely.

But, a few minutes later, when he looked up, he saw his daughter. He saw Fumiko, who had worked so hard to find him and the story of Hana. And he saw the expectant faces of all those Japanese children for whom Hana had become so important, so alive.

George realized that, in the end, one of Hana's wishes *had* come true. Hana had become a teacher. Because of her — her suitcase and her story — thousands of Japanese children were learning about what George believed to be the most important values in the world: tolerance, respect, and compassion. What a gift Fumiko and the children have given me, he thought. And what honor they have given Hana.

Fumiko asked the children to sit in a circle. She beamed with pride as, one by one, they presented George with their drawings and poems about Hana. When they had finished, Maiko stood up, took a deep breath, and read a poem aloud.

Hana Brady, thirteen years old, was the owner of this suitcase.
Fifty-five years ago, May 18, 1942 — two days after Hana's eleventh birthday — she was taken to Terezin in Czechoslovakia.
October 23, 1944, crowded into the freight train, she was sent to Auschwitz.

She was taken to the gas chamber right after.
People were allowed to take only one suitcase with them.
I wonder what Hana put in her suitcase.
Hana would have been sixty-nine years old today, but
her life stopped when she was thirteen.
I wonder what kind of girl she was.
A few drawings she made at Terezin — these are the
only things she left for us.
What do these drawings tell us?
Happy memories of her family?
Dreams and hopes for the future?
Why was she killed?
There was one reason.
She was born Jewish.
Name: Hana Brady. Date of Birth: May 16, 1931. Orphan.
We, Small Wings, will tell every child in Japan what
happened to Hana.
We, Small Wings, will never forget what happened to
one-and-a-half-million Jewish children.
We children can make a difference in building peace
in the world — so that the Holocaust will never
happen again.

By Small Wings, December 2000, Tokyo, Japan.
Translated from Japanese by Fumiko Ishioka.

While Maiko reads on the left, members of the Small Wings hold up signs saying "Let's Learn, Think and Act [to create peace] for the 21st century."

Afterword

The story of *Hana's Suitcase* continues to hold surprises for us. On a trip to Poland in March 2004, George and Fumiko learned that Hana's original suitcase was destroyed, along with many other objects from the Holocaust, in a suspicious fire in Birmingham, England in 1984.

The museum at Auschwitz created a replica — or copy — of the suitcase from a photograph. It was that replica which Fumiko and the Small Wings received in Tokyo. As a matter of policy Auschwitz tells borrowers when an object on loan is not the original. This time a mistake was made. George and Fumiko did not know that the suitcase was a replica until the recent trip to Poland.

On reflection, everyone involved is grateful that the curators at Auschwitz went to the trouble of creating a faithful replica of the suitcase. Without it, Fumiko would never have searched for Hana. She would never have found George. And we would never have the story of *Hana's Suitcase*.

Hana's Suitcase is now being read around the world by hundreds of thousands of children, in more than forty languages. Fumiko, George and the suitcase continue to travel, sharing Hana's story, the lessons of history and a message of tolerance.

Acknowledgments

FIRST AND FOREMOST, my thanks go to George Brady and Fumiko Ishioka. This is their story. Each of them, with remarkable dedication and generosity, helped to bring the book together. They are very tenacious and compassionate people, driven by the desire to make the world a better place, and to bring attention and honor to the memory of Hana Brady. I salute them.

My heart jumped the first time I learned of Hana's suitcase in an article by Paul Lungen in the *Canadian Jewish News*. The story so touched me that I decided to come out of "exile" and produce my first radio documentary in a dozen years. The result was "Hana's Suitcase," which aired on *The Sunday Edition* on CBC Radio One in January 2001.

The first phone call I received after the broadcast came from a tearful Margie Wolfe, who said right then and there that I had to write this book. Margie is one of my favorite people in the whole world — a fiercely loyal friend, and a hilarious, kooky, exuberantly talented woman whom I can now refer to as "my publisher" with feigned nonchalance.

Along with Margie, Sarah Swartz brought a clear and gentle touch to the editorial process. Jeffrey Canton, as well as the women of Second Story Press, Carolyn Foster and Laura McCurdy, also made important contributions. Reynold Gonsalves knows that without his patience and skill in the radio studio and on the computer, my life would be much more complicated than it already is. Thank you also to Carmelita Tenerife for her sustaining care and Teresa Brady for her kindness.

My sensational women friends were morale boosters, babysitters, and all-round hand holders in this writing project: Susanne Boyce, Cate Cochran, Joy Crysdale, Brooke Forbes, Francine Pelletier, Geraldine Sherman and Talin Vartanian. I want to give special thanks to 9-year-old Madeline Cochran for being an early reader of the manuscript. Her (and her mother's) suggestions were great!

No daughter could ask for more support and cheerleading from her parents. My mother, Helen, and my father, Gil, taught me (among many other things) to celebrate human struggle, to know the past and to fight for a better future. And they gave me the best big sister, Ruthie Tamara, who has encouraged me in every way.

Michael Enright — my beau and co-vivant — thought I could write a book long before I did, and never missed an opportunity to tell me so. His confidence in me, and his unvarnished enthusiasm about this project, terrified and thrilled me at the same time. At every step, he gave me the nourishment I wanted, the prodding I needed and the room to work. I am truly grateful for it all. I am also grateful for the true-heartedness of the Enright brood — Daniel, Anthony and Nancy.

My son — Gabriel Zev Enright Levine — is six years old now, too young to know Hana's story. But when he is old enough, I'll read it to him. I hope he will be as drawn to Hana, George and Fumiko as I was. I also hope he will learn from the story that history matters, and that despite the most unspeakable evil, good people and good deeds can make a difference.

—Karen Levine, 2002

Hana's Suitcase
Anniversary Album

Karen Levine, George Brady, and Fumiko Ishioka with the suitcase.

A Remarkable Decade
Karen Levine

I remember the moment I first read about the old brown suitcase in an article in a community newspaper. My knees wobbled. My heart thumped. I knew right away that this was an amazing story, but I never could have guessed how my life — and countless other lives — would be so changed by it.

I became interested in the Holocaust when I was in elementary school. Every Sunday morning, my dad would take me to a delicatessen for a treat, and Mrs. Kardish was always at the counter to serve us. On the inside of her forearm was a blue number. I don't remember how, but I learned that the number had been burned into her skin when she was in a concentration camp during the Second World War. I was too shy to ask her about it, but I was fascinated and unsettled by it.

When I was thirteen, my family traveled to Europe and one of the places we visited was the Buchenwald concentration camp, a place where thousands and thousands of Jews died. I'll never forget seeing the piles of shoes, human hair, glasses, leg braces — and the suitcases — in the museum there. After that trip, I was obsessed with the history of the Holocaust and read everything I could get my hands on. It was then that I started to tell stories and write about it. In my twenties, I went to work at the Canadian Broadcasting Corporation (CBC) and made a number of radio programs about the Holocaust.

I suppose I was trying to understand how such evil could have been allowed to happen. Six million Jews were murdered. Millions of others too: Roma, disabled people, people of color, gay people, communists, Slavs. The Holocaust made me angry — and sad. And because I am Jewish, I carried with me the frightening truth that if I'd been born in a different place, at a different time, it might have been me, or my family, who died with so many others.

Then in December 2000, I had that wobbly, heart-thumping moment when I learned about the suitcase and Hana, Fumiko, and George. Theirs was such an unusual story, such a strange combination of tragedy and hope. Three continents. Three generations. A mystery, pitfalls, setbacks, coincidences, and small miracles. A story from the past directly connected to the present.

That very night I found George's phone number and called him. He was happy to talk to me and said that Fumiko was about to arrive in Canada. It would be their first meeting. I was lucky to spend time with each of them, and later, I made a radio documentary called *Hana's Suitcase*. Six months after that, I started to write the book.

Shortly after the book was published, I received my very first letter from a young reader named Junior. It was thrilling! His teacher told me he'd had some rough times in his life, and some troubles with reading, but he carried *Hana's Suitcase* with him wherever he went. I paid a visit to his class. That was the first time I saw the powerful impact of the story on young readers.

Things began to snowball. In short order, I went from being a shy, behind-the-scenes person to speaking in huge auditoriums and theaters all over the world. It was exciting and really scary. I spent a lot of time in schools and I loved being with kids. Their natural sense of justice, their joy, bravery, and spontaneity gave me — give me — jolts of hope. Young readers connect the story of Hana to things that go on in their own schoolyards, where a brown kid, a gay kid, a disabled kid may be taunted simply because of who he or she is. They tell me that maybe next time they won't stand by and watch it happen. They are shocked by the idea that intolerance and racism can mean that children lose their families; that it has deadly consequences. And they love the notion — thanks to Fumiko and Small Wings — that kids can make a difference.

I am very grateful for the time I have spent with the story and with Fumiko and George. I have especially loved meeting young readers of the book. As I write this, I'm recalling so many of your faces, your challenging questions, your big hearts. The energy, honesty, and thought you have given to your thousands of letters, school projects, artwork, creative writing, and music is simply...wonderful.

There is one child — Hana Brady — who will never know the impact she has had on me and so many of you. I hope you'll never forget Hana or George or Fumiko and the lessons their story holds. It's very important to know about the past and to struggle — in our own ways, in our own corners of the world — for a more just and tolerant future. Thanks to you, I think *Hana's Suitcase* is in good hands.

All the best to each of you. And keep reading!

Karen Levine, 2012

Author, Karen Levine

Karen and publisher, Margie Wolfe,
after attending the Paris Book Fair in France.

Fumiko Ishioka

When Hana's suitcase arrived from Auschwitz in 2000, to tell you the truth, I didn't know what to do with it. How could I use this one empty suitcase to show what happened in such an enormous tragedy as the Holocaust? As I was looking at the name written on the suitcase, I became sure of one thing. I wanted to make this suitcase a symbol of life, not of the death of an unknown child. Small Wings students and I wanted to see the face of Hana. This is why I started the search.

So where would I go to look for Hana Brady? At first I wasn't sure. But once you start something there are always people out there who will help you. This is what I found out. It was a journey full of mixed emotions. It was heartbreaking when I learned of the fate of little, innocent Hana. What struck me more was the pain her big brother George must have felt all these years after losing her. The moment I saw the face of Hana in the picture George sent us, which is now on the cover of the book, all I had in my mind was George's deep sorrow. But George's story didn't end there. As you have read, he now has a new, beautiful family of his own in Canada. That was the biggest and the happiest surprise at the end of my search.

George is my true hero. Because he shared with us his most difficult memories, despite his sorrow, Hana's suitcase was able to start a new journey, sharing the lessons of history. Every time I meet George, he has a new story to tell from his survival in Auschwitz. I have been fortunate to learn from his example of never giving up. His courage, generosity, and optimism in life have been so inspiring.

How wonderful to have been able to share the story, through this book, with so many more people globally! On the tenth anniversary of its publication, I would like to express my appreciation to Karen and Margie.

Hana's Suitcase opened the door, for me and for the story, to a whole new world. Every time I receive letters and e-mails from readers, I feel like I have so many friends across the globe working together to fight intolerance and prejudice so this world can be a better place. My goal is to travel with Hana's suitcase all over Japan to continue sharing the story of Hana and George. If we can see what's in this one empty suitcase, I believe we can use the same imagination and compassion to understand the fate of another child who suffered under the brutal Japanese occupation during WWII, or the pain of any other child who is, at this moment, being affected in war-torn areas, or even a neighbor who is being bullied and hurt right next to us in school.

Students of Small Wings have now all graduated from the group. Maiko is a kindergarten teacher. Mirai is a cook working hard to open her own restaurant. Akira is studying engineering and has a dream of traveling into space. I am in touch with Hisano, Ikuno, Saori, Sakiko, Nanako — all of them — and hope to have a reunion soon to celebrate the tenth anniversary.

Hana's suitcase is indeed, no longer empty. It is filled, not just with sad memories, but also with life and hope for the future.

All the best,

Fumiko Ishioka
Tokyo Holocaust Education
Resource Center, 2012

*Fumiko and George in
Taber, Alberta in 2003.*

In 2005, Karen was thrilled to visit Japan.

RIGHT AND BOTTOM: Fumiko has continued to visit schools throughout Japan — 800 of them at last count.

George Brady

It has been over sixty-seven years since I last saw my beloved sister, Hana. I have thought about her every day, and of the life she might have led had she survived the war. Over fifteen years ago, I returned to Auschwitz hoping to close the door on the pain and loss I felt over losing my entire family. I went there with my youngest child, Lara Hana. We had no idea that this would be the beginning of a new chapter for Hana and our family.

Just two years later, we received a letter from Japan, inviting us to meet Small Wings, a group of children dedicated to world peace, who were fascinated by Hana's story. You know what happened from there. Fumiko's work with Small Wings at the Tokyo Holocaust Education Research Center has transformed the tragedy of Hana's fate into a lesson for Japanese children. Karen Levine and Margie Wolfe have shared this journey with us from Fumiko's first visit to Toronto, and with their help we have been able to spread the story. Now families around the world write to us, letting us know that *Hana's Suitcase* is a book they read, reread, and share.

This story has been documented in the book you now hold in your hands, on stage, and on screen and has been told in many languages to millions of children. Lara and I have spoken at schools across Canada, the United States, throughout Europe, Asia, South America, and Africa, sharing Hana's story and the message of tolerance and peace. We have been greatly moved by the enthusiasm and empathy of the children we've met, and have great hope that stories like Hana's can be prevented in the future.

Until Fumiko's letter arrived, my sole confidantes outside of my family were fellow survivors. Closest among them was Kurt Kotouc, who was the final link in Fumiko's quest to find me. Kurt did not have an easy life after the war when the communists rolled into Czechoslovakia, yet he never gave up on keeping the memory of the lost children alive, even so many years after their deaths. He always took particular delight in our reports of where *Hana's Suitcase* was shared and who played him in the various stage performances! His final contribution was an interview he did for the documentary just weeks before his death. That I was able to take this part of our journey with Kurt, is particularly important.

Children often ask what Fumiko is like, and now I finally get the chance to give you the honest truth: She has been a part of the Brady Family from the moment she arrived at our Toronto home. We've traveled together speaking to children, we've taken vacations together, and she now gives me as much trouble as my children, Doug, Paul, David, and Lara! Despite the misbehaving and giggling that the girls get up to, I'm thrilled that they are such great friends and equally dedicated to spreading Hana's message. In 2010, Lara and Fumiko went without me to South Africa and Australia, and I was delighted to hear about how the children there were able to relate some of their own histories and experiences to the injustices Hana and I faced as children. It never fails to amaze me that young people everywhere, dealing with loss, bullying, and serious hardships are still full of hope, and how they are inspired by *Hana's Suitcase* to take a stand against injustice. Despite the crazy schedules and amount of work involved, children like this — who remind me of Hana — make our efforts worthwhile. I am delighted that Lara and Fumiko will continue telling Hana's story long after I retire my passport.

And don't worry. It's not all work when we travel. As bossy as they may be, the girls always make time for me to taste local ice cream and visit aquariums in the cities we visit. So please, keep sending us recommendations!

When I came back to Nové Město na Moravě after the war, I was a young man of seventeen and the only survivor from my family. I was determined to put sadness behind me and change my life. Once again, I turned to Uncle

TOP AND RIGHT: George, Fumiko, and Lara visited Scotland in 2012

Fumiko and Lara relax with a friend in Australia after a tour where they met with over 5,000 students.

Ludvik and Aunt Heda for advice. They encouraged me to make a fresh start in Canada. Now, when I travel back to visit my cousin Vera, we are continually astounded by the impact that Hana has had. What pleases Vera most is that Hana's dream of becoming a teacher was realized.

The Brady family has not been forgotten in Nové Město na Moravě. Our house and the shop my parents ran are now occupied by other families and businesses. But ask anyone in town where the Brady store or the Brady house is, and they will point you in the right direction. The house is now a historic site with a commemorative plaque to Hana outside and a photo museum dedicated to our family inside. The house is even part of a geo-cache hunt, so tourists can follow clues around our town, which will eventually lead them to a hidden geo-cache treasure.

Knowing that even though her life was cut short, Hana has managed to teach millions of children about acceptance and compassion is an unbelievable gift. I have come to believe that our story speaks for those

123

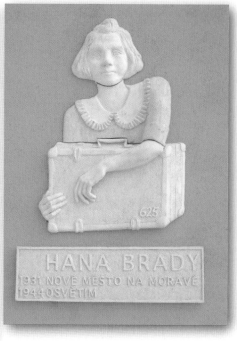

The Brady family's home still stands in the town square. Now it bears a plaque commemorating Hana and houses a photo museum dedicated to the Bradys.

who had no one to speak for them. I have entrusted Fumiko and Lara with sharing our experience with future generations and I hope that Hana may continue to speak for the millions whose stories could never be told.

Bringing to life a story that began over eighty years ago is not an easy task. Karen has done this with such grace that children relate to Hana as though she were a friend. The extent of their reaction renews my faith in how one person can change millions of lives. My little sister was murdered at thirteen, but her life continues to resonate seven decades after that fact.

Finally, to the young readers of our book, you have the desire and the opportunity to create a better world. I cannot emphasize enough the importance of family, freedom, compassion, and respect for others. I hope Hana's tragedy encourages you to explore history in order to learn more about the consequences of hatred and intolerance and to take an active stand against injustice.

All my best wishes,

George Brady & Family

P.S. On the tenth anniversary of the book, I'd like to answer the most common question Lara and I are asked: Did you ever find the bottle? We did, in fact, go looking for the bottle during the filming of *Inside Hana's Suitcase*. Unfortunately, after almost seventy years, property lines have shifted and changes have been made. The bottle is likely buried forever. In all honesty, I prefer it that way, as Hana had always planned to dig it up again after the war. I like to think that maybe the bottle is still waiting for us to find together.

Before the Suitcase: Memories of Hana

Despite the years that have passed, Nové Město na Moravě still counts the Brady family as one of their own. Locals refer to the yellow house on the main square as "U Brady" (at the Bradys'), and elderly citizens are keen to share their recollections of Hana and her family in the days before the Holocaust. George recently asked a few friends to tell their stories, and they wrote, reflecting on happier times when neighbors were unafraid to support each other regardless of religion or social status.

Alena Kopackova

"I am over eighty years old, which makes me one of the keepers of memories… Our town was never large; we all knew each other. My parents knew the whole Brady family very well, and when time permitted, we visited each other as friends…One meeting place was the Harusaka cottage, a destination for hiking excursions. The tenant of the cottage set up a swing for us between the tall trees, and it was paradise.

"You could go very high on the swing, but you could go even higher if you stood up on the seat. That was forbidden, but I did it all the same. My brother Pavel pushed me, and I flew! But I had new soles on my shoes, and at the highest point of the swing I slipped, lost hold of the rope, and fell among the roots of the trees.

"Pavel ran into the cottage shouting that I'd killed myself. Dad ran, but Mr. Brady was the first to reach me. He took me in his arms and put me into [his] car, and he took Dad and me to the doctor. I had the wind knocked out of me, a huge bruise on my bottom, a bloody nose, and scratches. In a week everything was fine, but my family always gratefully remembered that each day during that week, the Bradys sent someone from the store to ask how I was doing."

Dr. Marta Latalova

"Though we never spoke directly about it, I knew how [Hana] suffered because of the yellow star she had to wear, but even so, we sometimes went for walks together through the town.

"Often, when my five grandchildren ask me 'Granny, what was it like when you were young?' I tell them about Hanicka, and by their reactions, I know they will tell her story to their children as well. I think all of us who have memories of these sad events should do the same, so that we will never again have to hear, or tolerate hearing, the remark that 'the Holocaust wasn't really all that bad.'"

TOP: *After her parents were taken away by the Nazis, Hana (in front) lived with Aunt Heda, Uncle Ludvik, and their daughter Vera.*
BOTTOM: *Vera and George today.*

Alena Blahova-Nemeckova

"…we often snuck into the garden of [our teacher] Mr. Kleveta…The gate to his garden was in our street, and he never locked it. We spent pleasant times there by the pond. In the corner was a beehive, which was our teacher's pride and joy. We were so absorbed in our childish problems that often our teacher surprised us. But he was very fond of Hana, and he never scolded us for visiting his garden without permission. He knew very well that wherever Hana was, there would be no trouble.

"During the occupation, when the Jews were forbidden from attending classes, Hana would walk past the school in the afternoons. Mr. Kleveta would expect her, and he would say 'Quick! Go to the window and give a little wave to Hanicka.' And he would stand by the doorway so we wouldn't be caught doing it."

Hana is in the top row, 5th from the right in this class photo. It was taken before she was forced to leave school because she was Jewish.

Libuse Minarikova

"In the third grade, our classmate, Hanicka, stopped coming to school. The reason given was that she was Jewish. It was the first time I ever had heard that word, and I didn't understand what it meant because [to me] they were people like everyone else. The last time I saw Hanicka, she was on the corner by the school. She was wearing a gray coat with a yellow star on the front. She was saying goodbye. We didn't understand, and probably neither did she, what was going on or what was to come. In the summer of 1962, I visited the Holocaust Museum in Auschwitz. The horrors of the concentration camp came home to me when, on a pile of suitcases belonging to the murdered prisoners, I saw Hana's suitcase."

Hana and George, pictured above when they were very young, came from a close family. When the children weren't helping out in the Brady store, they often went on picnics and bicycle rides in the country. That's Hana bringing up the rear.

Wonderful Letters

Hana's Suitcase has sparked a flood of heartfelt letters to Karen, Fumiko, and George from young readers. This tiny sampling only begins to demonstrate the feelings and thoughts the book evokes. The common thread seems to be that it speaks directly to every child and makes connections to their present lives as well as to the past.

January 19, 2010

Dear Mr. Brady,

My name is Kristen and I am thirteen years old. I am in grade eight. I live in Eskasoni, a very small community, with the population of 3,500 people. I have read the book *Hana's Suitcase* and it has inspired me to write this letter. I thank you very much for all the lessons I learned from *Hana's Suitcase*. It breaks my heart to know that you went to two Concentration Camps.

I am very glad to be able to write to you. Mr. Brady, I may not know you, and I do not know how it feels to have witnessed what you went through, but you are a Hero to us! You are a very brave and valiant man. I am a young Mi'kmaq person, a minority group from the First Nations, and because of whom we are, we see racism and witness hatred and social injustices.

I could some what relate to you because once, the Mi'kmaq people were killed by the Europeans. They wanted to get rid of us. They were giving us gifts, such as blankets and other things that were filled with Small Pox. They knew that the Mi'kmaq people would get sick. The Europeans just wanted the Mi'kmaq people's land, but nothing could really relate as much for what happened to the Jewish people. You're a very special person to me because you survived the Holocaust that was a very crucial event.

Once again, I would like to thank you for this opportunity. I am very proud of myself for writing this letter and getting to read *Hana's Suitcase*. How could I ever thank you enough for taking your time to read this letter? You're one in a million Mr. Brady!

Sincerely,

Kristen

Dear Mr. Brady,

I'm Emily and I'm 13-years-old. I've just read "Hana's Suitcase", the story of Ms. Fumiko Ishioka's adventure to uncover the tale behind your sistere's suitcase.

It makes me awfully mad to think how cruel the humankind can be. And how stupid we can be at times. Most say that Adolf Hitler was responsible for this whole thing. That he had a very twisted mind. I disagree. Sure, he had a very big part in it, but this wasn't a one-man show. The question is, why did common people listen to such a man? Of course he had authority, but didn't most people know right from wrong? How could one turn against his own neighbours like the way many did to the Jews?

World War II is one of the saddest periods in history. Hitler's treatment to the Jews was simply unjustice. Jews did nothing more than be in the wrong place at the wrong time! And they are the ones suffering so badly. It's so ... WRONG — aren't all wars?

Yet now, decades after that terror, the politicians are doing it again. The war with Iraq now. It's differently from WWII, but so similiar too. Now they are doing what was done to Jews to the Muslims. Didn't people learn anything from the past wars? Did all that really happen for nothing?

130

I believe that history happens for a reason —
to teach the future generation a lesson — in was
not to do as well as what to do.

And I'm so glad that you shared your
memories with the public, for it did teach
me lots.

It must be hard to bring back those
memories of such loss — I cannot imagine.
But you must know that your part
of the story plays a very important role in
this lesson — to the Japanese children as well as
people like me, readers.

I can relate a little to Hana's story
through my reading, not much, though. I truly
wish to understand it more. Is there more
to this war?

I'd really like to hear the story from
you. And your story in more details, how
you got on in this strange, new country. That
I could relate to. I went through coming here, not
able to communicate at all, only over three years
ago. I came from China and was horribly miserable
the first month here. But I cannot imagine
your story — coming here with a memory like your
own.

But would you share your tale with me?
The one of your new beginning.

Thank you for taking time to read my
letter. And thank you for Hana's story.

Yours sincerely,

Emily

April, 2003

A wonderful lesson Learned

I felt terribly sad when Hana and George were separated, because I always say my sister is annoying and that I wish I didn't have a sister. But I really would be sad If we were separated.

This story changed the way I act towords my sister, and I feel alot better than I did, after I'm finished talking with her.

Thank you very much for making me and my sister feel Good!

from, Sarah

March 2, 2007

Dear Ms. Levine,

Well I don't know where to get started. I really hate reading, but when I read your book I really enjoyed reading your book. I liked it because I had the same experience like the Holocaust. Tears came down my eyes because Hannah was a little girl that didn't do anything-wrong. Her life ended at an early age and she didn't fulfill the dreams she had.

My name is Njomza. I'm from Eastern Europe. I've had the same experience as Hannah Brady did. I can't tell you or show you how much this book opened my eyes to reading. I see now that one page of a book can take you back fifty years and show you what people went through during the Holocaust! I'm really overwhelmed and don't know how to put this in writing, but your book made a difference to my life. If it wasn't for my wonderful English teacher telling me to give this book a try I would never be writing you this letter. I'm really thankful that you have the nerves to tell us about horrible things that happened in the past. I wish more authors like you put great time and effort in their work and gave wonderful descriptions in each and every page. So thank you a lot, for making one book change my life for ever, and change my mind about books.

Love Yours Truly,

Njomza

Karen Levine
P.O. Box 500, Station „A"
Toronto, Ontario
Canada
MSW 1E6

Dear Ms Levine

At the Leipzig Book Trade Fair you were so exceedingly kind to give me a copy of
your excellent radio documentary „Hana's Suitcase". I want to thank you very much
for it. (I am very sorry that I did not write much sooner, but in the meantime I had to
translate a 200 hundred pages book within less than two months and was awfully
busy. I also found it difficult to express the following thoughts in English.)
„Hana's Suitcase" has become very important to me and my family. After I came
home from Leipzig, my husband, my daughter Franziska and I listened to the
documentary first thing in the morning. We were deeply moved by it, to hear how
George and Fumiko tried hard to tell about Hana without showing too much emotion
and were overwhelmed by their feelings.
I am very glad that your book was translated into German because we Germans have
the obligation to face our past. The Holocaust is dealt thoroughly in German schools.
However, I think that when learning about an individual person who was murdered
in the Holocaust one can come closer to understanding what an enormous crime that
was than by just being confronted with the historical facts and those unimaginably
high numbers of people who were murdered. If people come to know what the
Holocaust did to an individual person they will want to learn more about the
Holocaust. A German child or adolescent who reads your book will feel the need to
learn about the past and will not be prone to antisemitic ideas.
Franziska read „Anne Frank's Diary" a while ago, as I had when I was her age. But I
always thought that „Anne Frank's Diary" might appeal to girls rather than to boys.
Your book now fills this gap. My son Leopold did not go out playing until he had
finished reading „Hanas Koffer". Leopold is twelve years old and wants to be cool,
but he told me: „Mummy, I had to cry all the time, it's so sad." He is so impressed by
your book that he very often talks about Hana and George and told his two younger
sisters, to whom I have not read the book yet, many details about Hana and George.
I do hope that very many people will read your book and learn about Hana, how she
lived and how she was murdered. I can assure you that not only George Brady's
family will never forget Hana, but that we will neither. And I cannot image that
anybody who reads your book will be able to forget Hana.
I am very grateful to you, George Brady and Fumiko Ishioka for making Hana's life
and death known to the public.

Yours sincerely

Christiane

I know how Hana feels without having parents because I'm a orfin too. It would be pretty hard having to be a jewish girl in those times. George is veri lucky to be alive.

Tia, Taber, Alberta, 2001

Without telling this story again Hanna would just be — one of the many children that died. Since this book was written Hanna has become a face inside of everyone who has read the book.

Jonathan, Winnipeg, Manitoba, 2003

Everyone should know about what you went through. They need to know it's real and still happens today. People might not care because it was so long ago but they should care! I guess what I'm trying to say is I care.

Jeremy, Trenton, Ontario, 2003

The Story of Two Quilts

In September 2005, my beautiful daughter, Alicia, started Grade 4 at Gander Academy in Gander, Newfoundland. For the next two months, everything pertaining to school was all about the book *Hana's Suitcase* and the wonderful quilt the children were making as a gift for the author when she came to visit. Unfortunately, Alicia, who was born with quadra spastic athetoid cerebral palsy, had an uncontrollable seizure on November 23 that eventually caused her brain and vital organs to shut down. Despite the efforts of the Janeway Children's Hospital in St. John's and the Hospital for Sick Children in Toronto, Alicia passed away five days later.

About a week after her funeral service, the principal of Gander Academy told me the Grade 4 students and the staff were planning a celebration of her life at the school, and they had special things they wanted to present to me. On that occasion, there was much talk about how much Alicia loved *Hana's Suitcase*. Being a child with disabilities, she knew how hard it was to be restricted from doing the things you love, so she could relate to Hana. Like Hana, Alicia loved her life and never lost her determination. Her teacher, Ms. Morawski, then informed me that she had spoken with the book's author and had told her about Alicia's love for the book and about her passing. Together, they determined that the original quilt, which included a panel made by Alicia, should be presented to me in memory of Alicia and that the class would make another quilt to give to the author when she came to visit.

I would like to say thank you for this wonderful book and for giving my daughter joy. My beautiful quilt with the panel made by Alicia is something I will treasure always.

—Sherry Norman

Alicia Norman

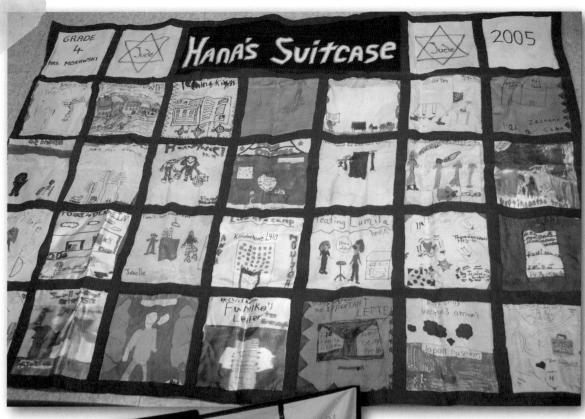

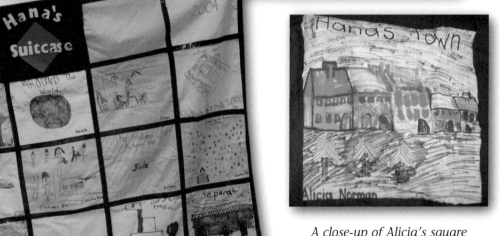

A close-up of Alicia's square

At the top is the original quilt made by the Grade 4 students of Gander Academy. They made a second quilt (bottom) and presented it to Karen.

Ten Years on the Move

As the amazing story of Hana's suitcase spread, Karen, Fumiko, George, and later George's daughter, Lara Hana, were welcomed in schools, community centers, churches, and at conferences in many countries around the world, underlining the book's ability to speak to people of all origins and ages. They have visited children in Japan, Canada, USA (twenty schools in one month!), South Africa, Mexico, Scotland, France, Italy, Israel, Germany, England, Australia, and New Zealand.

Whenever they travel, George, Fumiko, and Karen find the welcome mat — and sign — out. This one is from Mount Hebron School in New Jersey, USA.

Leo Pavlát, Director of the Jewish Museum in Prague, presents a copy of Hana's Suitcase to Michelle Obama after her tour of the city's Jewish Ghetto on April 5, 2009.

Karen, Fumiko, and Maiko from the Small Wings group were in Toronto for the launch of Hana's Suitcase *in 2002.*

Hana's Suitcase *was featured at the International Book Fair of Torino, Italy…*

…and again at the Salon du livre in Montreal.

Fumiko, George, and Karen pose with the suitcase and students of Palos South Middle School in Palos Park, Illinois, 2003.

Enthusiastic students proudly hold their books as they get a closer look at the well-traveled suitcase in Mexico, 2007.

Fumiko and Lara are given a very warm welcome by Australian schoolgirls in 2010.

George and Fumiko meet young Israeli friends in 2005.

Fumiko and Lara take the suitcase to South Africa in 2008.

Young Canadian fans wave the flag and celebrate the arrival of the suitcase to their school in Perth, Ontario in 2003.

Awards and Honors

No other Canadian children's book has won as many awards as Hana's Suitcase. *Shown below are just a few of them: The Silver Birch Award, the UNICEF Paolo Ungari Prize, the Hackmatack Children's Choice Award, The Red Cedar Award, and the Golden Oak Award.*

Canadian Awards

- 2003 CLA Book of the Year Award for Children
- 2003 Ontario Library Association Silver Birch Award
- 2003 The Golden Oak Book Award
- 2003 Helen and Stan Vine Canadian Jewish Book Award
- 2003 Children's Literature Roundtables of Canada Information Book Award
- 2003 CNIB Tiny Torgi Literary Award
- 2003 National Chapter of Canada IODE Violet Downey Book Award
- 2004 Alberta Children's Choice Rocky Mountain Book Award
- 2004 Hackmatack Children's Choice Book Award

- 2004-2005 Red Cedar Book Award Non-Fiction
- Canadian Children's Book Centre Children's Choice
- IBBY Honor List

American Awards

- 2002 Sydney Taylor Book Award
- 2003 Special Recognition Award, National Jewish Book Awards, Jewish Book Council
- 2004 Flora Stieglitz Straus Award for Nonfiction, Bank Street College
- 2004 Best Children's Books of the Year, Bank Street College
- 2004 Capitol Choice
- 2004 IRA Children's Book Award Notable: Intermediate Nonfiction
- 2004 Notable Social Studies Trade Book for Young People, NCSS-CBC
- 2004 Notable Children's Book (ALA-ALSC)
- 2004 Notable Book for a Global Society, International Reading Association
- Teachers' Choices for 2004 — International Reading Association
- 2005 Skipping Stones Honor Award
- 2006 Great Lakes Great Books Award Winner
- 2007 Rebecca Caudill Young Readers' Book Award Master List
- Winner of a Parent's Guide Children's Media Award

143

An Amazing Celebration: The Silver Birch Day

Every year across Canada, students, teachers, and librarians gear up for the excitement of the children's choice awards. Kids get to pick the winners! In 2003, Hana's Suitcase won every non-fiction children's choice award in the country.

Many of the first school visits I made in my home province of Ontario began when *Hana's Suitcase* was nominated for the Silver Birch Award. There are programs similar to the Silver Birch — children's choice awards — in other Canadian provinces and in many American states.

Every year the Ontario Library Association chooses ten fiction and ten non-fiction books. Eleven hundred schools across the province form reading clubs to assess the titles on those lists. Then fifty-five thousand children across Ontario vote for their favorite books, and the results are tallied.

In 2003, *Hana's Suitcase* was the winner for non-fiction. The day of celebration — when the results were announced — was truly one of the best days of my life. Fifteen hundred kids gathered in an outdoor amphitheater at Toronto's Harbourfront, all screaming their love of books. It was an absolutely beautiful sight. The event — such a wonderful representation of the potential and power of children — connected beautifully with one of the themes in *Hana's Suitcase*; that children, given half a chance, can make a difference in the world.

I'll never forget the moment that our book was declared the winner. I locked eyes with my son — then seven — who was beyond ecstatic and, of course, with George who — by the time I found him in that gorgeous sea of faces — was weeping. I asked him to come up and stand with me on the stage as I read my acceptance speech. It was a thrilling and moving event for all of us and one we will always remember.

But the most amazing thing to come out of the Silver Birch was this. A teacher from one of Toronto's suburbs took me aside to tell me proudly that every single member of her reading club had voted for *Hana's Suitcase*. Not only that, she said eighty per cent of the kids in the club were Muslim. Even now, I get goose bumps remembering that. It reminds me that *Hana's Suitcase* is a story that seems to build bridges, not fences...that makes the struggle for peace and justice as compelling as the history of war.

—Karen Levine

Excitement ran high as voting students awaited the announcement of the winner.

Karen is moved by the reaction of the children.

Karen reads her Silver Birch acceptance speech as an emotional George looks on.

The Story Around the World

At last count, children in forty-five countries, including those who read Braille, know Hana's Suitcase. It is published, sometimes in several editions in: Argentina, Australia, Austria, Belgium, Brazil, Canada (English/French), Chile, China, Czech Republic, Denmark, England, France, Germany, Greece, Hungary, Iceland, India, Indonesia, Ireland, Israel, Italy, Japan, Korea, Mexico, New Zealand, Norway, Philippines, Poland, Portugal, Romania, Serbia, Slovakia, Slovenia, Spain, South Africa, Sweden, Taiwan, Thailand, The Netherlands, Turkey, Uruguay, USA (English/Spanish), and Wales.

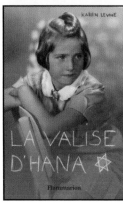

汉娜的手提箱

한나의 가방

Hana's Suitcase

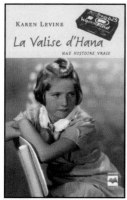

La Valise d'Hana
UNE HISTOIRE VRAIE

KAREN LEVINE

Karen Levine
Igaz történet...

ハンナ
かばん
アウシュビッツからのメッセージ

カレン・レビン／著 石岡史子／訳

Hana's Suitcase
by
Karen Levine
A TRUE STORY

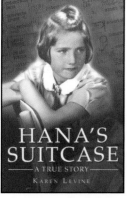

HANA'S
SUITCASE
A TRUE STORY
KAREN LEVINE

Karen Levine
A TRUE STORY
Read by Stephanie

Karen Levine
Jóðn saga

LA VALISE
D'HANA

KAREN LEVINE

LA VIE EN VRAI!   CASTOR POCHE

Hana's Koffer

Een waargebeurd
verhaal

Karen Levine

Karen Levine
A Mala de Hana
uma história verdadeira

Terramar

Hana's Suitcase
on Stage

Original story by
Karen Levine Emil Sher

Hana's Suitcase
by
Karen Levine
A TRUE STORY

Hana's Suitcase has been produced as a play in Canada, the USA, England, and Japan and as two documentaries for television as well as a feature-length documentary called Inside Hana's Suitcase.

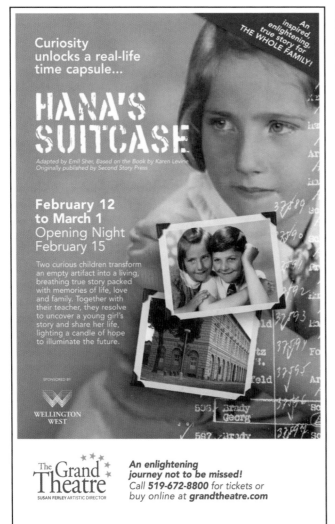

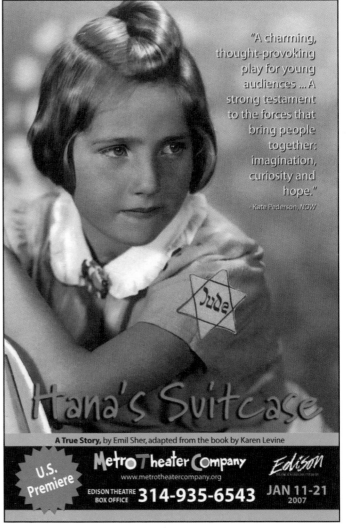

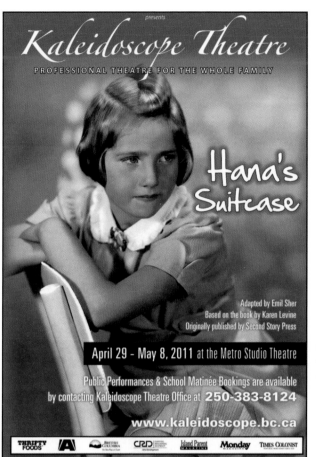

presents

Kaleidoscope Theatre
PROFESSIONAL THEATRE FOR THE WHOLE FAMILY

Hana's Suitcase

Adapted by Emil Sher
Based on the book by Karen Levine
Originally published by Second Story Press

April 29 - May 8, 2011 at the Metro Studio Theatre

Public Performances & School Matinée Bookings are available
by contacting Kaleidoscope Theatre Office at **250-383-8124**

www.kaleidoscope.bc.ca

המזוודה של חנה

הצגה מאת
אמיל שר
על-פי ספרה רב המכר
של קארן לוין

סיפור אמיתי, מטלטל ומפתיע, שנוגע ללבם של מיליוני
אנשים ברחבי העולם.

מסע מרתק בעקבות מזוודה מסתורית של הילדה חנה ברידי שחיה בתקופת
השואה, המלמד כי גם איווע טראאני יכול לנשר תקוה לעתיד טוב יותר.

בכורה ישראלית

יוזמה והפקה: תיאטרון הנפש
תרגום ועיבוד: בֵּאטְרִיס הָל
בימוי: הווארד ריף

יום רביעי 14.4.2010
בשעות 17:30 ו-19:30, במדיטק חולון

פרטים ורכישת כרטיסים: **03-5021552**

תיאטרון הנפש
עיריית תל אביב - יפו   משרד התרבות
www.nepheshtheatre.co.il

Hana's suitcase

— A true story

Adapted by Emil Sher
Based on the book
by Karen Levine
Originally published by
Second Story Press

"A charming, thought-
provoking play for
young audiences...A
strong testament to the
forces that bring people
together: imagination,
curiosity and hope."
— NOW Magazine

READ THE BOOK, SEE
THE PLAY, MEET THE
AUTHOR

Join our Community Read,
in partnership with the Harry &
Rose Samson Family Jewish
Community Center, around Hana's
Suitcase book and visit their events.
visit mmjccmke.org
for details.

Media Sponsor
FOX 6

September 14 – October 7, 2007

TICKETS ON SALE AUGUST 24! CALL TODAY! (414) 273-7206 • FIRSTSTAGE.ORG

FIRST STAGE CHILDREN'S THEATER – Todd Wehr Theater, Marcus Center for the Performing Arts

Magnus THEATRE   Go Live

HANA'S SUITCASE

ADAPTED BY
EMIL SHER
BASED ON THE BOOK BY
KAREN LEVINE
ORIGINALLY PUBLISHED BY SECOND STORY PRESS

REBECCA ARENA, CHRIS COCHE
MEAGHAN AMY MYERS
AVA WEINBERG, BRIAN YOUNG
ANDREW YU, VIVIANA ZARRILLO

Directed by
MARIO CRUDO

MARCH 3 - 19, 2011
BOX OFFICE: 345-5552

WWW.MAGNUS.ON.CA

This poster is for the feature length documentary,
Inside Hana's Suitcase, *a Rhombus Media/In Film Praha production.*

Things You Can Do

Over the last ten years, Hana's Suitcase *has inspired an extraordinary range of classroom projects. Kids and teachers have really used their imaginations! These activities have helped students to connect even more closely with Hana, George, and Fumiko, to explore the history of the Holocaust more deeply, and to grapple with some of the difficult questions and themes raised by the story.*

Here are just a few examples that you and your classmates might try.

1. Your own suitcase

Bring an old suitcase from home (or build one out of cardboard). Choose five objects to put in the suitcase — the things you would take with you if you were forced to leave your home the way Hana and George were. Think about why you chose each one, and write a paragraph about what that object means to you.

2. What does it look like?

- Make a poster or painting that illustrates a theme in the story.
- What does danger look like?
- What does safety look like?
- What does hatred look like?
- What does war look like?
- What does peace look like?

3. Write a letter to Hana

Imagine yourself to be one of the people in Hana's life — George, Uncle Ludvik, Boshka the housekeeper, Maria, Hana's school friend, Ella the girl in Theresiendstadt. Write a letter to Hana that tries to explain what is happening to her.

4. Do you have wings?

Think about pulling together your own Small Wings club, and come up with activities that help fight racism in your own community.

5. Connect with living history

Find out if there is a Holocaust survivor living near you. (Ask a teacher or parent to help with this.) Ask if he or she would be willing to come and talk to your class.

6. Connect with your own history

Use the story as a jumping off point to explore a difficult experience in your own family's past. Interview your parents, grandparents, or other relatives. Search for photographs. Do some research about the times. And then write it all up as a story — your own piece of history.

Here are some websites that might give you more ideas:

Social Justice Stories: www.socialjusticestories.com

The Brady family website: www.hanassuitcase.ca

Tokyo Holocaust Education Resource Center:

www.ne.jp/asahi/holocaust/tokyo

Karen's radio documentary: www.cbc.ca/thesundayedition/ documentaries/2009/09/01/hanas-suitcase

Film *Inside Hana's Suitcase*: www.insidehanassuitcase.com

Montreal Holocaust Memorial Center: www.mhmc.ca/en

Nové Město na Moravě in Moravia: www.nmnm.cz

Terezin Memorial: www.pamatnik-terezin.cz

Jewish Musem in Prague: www.jewishmuseum.cz

The State Museum of Auschwitz-Birkenau: www.auschwitz.org

Dear Ms. Levine,

I am a 12-year-old girl who read the book Hana's Suitcase and loved it. Hana and Fumiko's story really touched me, so I wanted to thank you for writing the book. I also wanted to tell you about my Bat Mitzvah project. Fumiko's dedication to educating children about the Holocaust inspired me, and so I wanted to help her with that mission. My mom and her friend Jill Felts, who owns a jewelry company, worked with me to design a necklace that I could sell to raise money for the Tokyo Holocaust Education Resource Center. I have enclosed one of them as a gift to you, since your book inspired the project. Thank you again for writing such an excellent book!

Sincerely,
Rachel Berger

P.S. — I'm sending charms to Fumiko Ishioka and George Brady too. I hope they get them!

Group and class projects are one way to make a difference, but many young people feel compelled to do something meaningful on their own in response to the story. One such person is Rachel Berger who undertook a very special Bat Mitzvah project.

153

The Feather Project...
One Angel at a Time

For teacher Wendy Alexis and her Grade 6 students at St. Luke Catholic School in Ottawa, Ontario, Hana's Suitcase resonated in a very meaningful and personal way, connecting history to modern times. Many of the students had come to Canada to seek refuge from hardship and persecution. This is their story.

When children are young, they love to hear stories. As they grow older, they want to tell them, especially their own.

Welcome to our Grade 6 class, a place where stories are treasured and trusted and told. And then, like magic, they transform us.

We will never forget one special day. It was in 2004 — April, in fact — when several stories converged to mark out a path for us. One was *Hana's Suitcase*, which we had recently read as part of a literary study of the Holocaust; another was the documentary *Paper Clips*; the third was a poetry unit we were working on. Two others concerned the upcoming tenth anniversary of the 1994 Rwandan genocide, as well as the personal testimony of Marie, a beautiful Rwandan child in our class.

As most of the students were either immigrants or refugees — many of them victims of war — it was not uncommon for them to discuss relatives or events from home, wherever in the world home happened to be.

When we asked our young friend from Rwanda why she never talked about the rest of her family there, she replied, "How can I? They're all dead. There's no one left."

Silence.

Nobody spoke. There was nothing to say. And then Marie, who had been silent so long, began to tell her story...and her country's. She talked, and we learned. Those lessons transfigured a classroom, changed our lives, and charted the course ahead.

154

Our class started writing. Wow, did we write! To commemorate the tenth anniversary of the genocide, we wrote to our school's Rwandan families who had survived the massacre. We wrote to Rwanda's Ambassador to Canada. We wrote to Lieutenant General Roméo Dallaire, who had commanded the UN troops there and had battled his own demons ever since. We wrote poetry. But writing wasn't enough; we needed to do more.

Then one day, after reading the final verse of one of our own poems...

So pluck a feather from their wings,
And keep it as a sign.
Remember those the world forgot
One angel at a time.

...the answer came to us. We would honor each victim — "one angel at a time" — with a feather, and we would ask some important people — world leaders — to contribute a single feather to launch our campaign. We wanted them to realize that if twelve-year-olds understood the lessons of genocide, then they had better remember them, too.

Soon mail began arriving from UN Secretary-General Kofi Annan, South Africa's Archbishop Desmond Tutu, Liberia's President Ellen Johnson-Sirleaf, former U.S. President Bill Clinton, and others. Following exposure from a CBC radio documentary entitled *One Angel at a Time*, we were flooded with thousands of feathers and letters from people who wanted to support us. To our delight, we even received feathers from *Hana's Suitcase* author, Karen Levine, and her son.

The rest is history, our class's history. Our precious cargo of more than 105,000 feathers is locked in an old blue steamer trunk, which is the centerpiece of our classroom. It, along with its stories, has become the legacy that each group of students passes on to the next.

Our hope is to create a life-sized tree — The Angels' Tree — from which our feathers will hang like leaves. It will be a testament to the delicate, but transcendent power of the human spirit — rooted in the earth, yet destined for the skies. When completed, our tree will be "transplanted" from our classroom to the Rwandan Embassy, a poignant reminder of a people the world forgot.

So, if someday in April,
You wander by our tree,
You'll hear each feather whispering,
"My name is _____ ;

...remember me..."

Between 1939 and 1945, one regime silenced eleven million voices — six million of them Jewish...one of them Hana's.

The true gift of *Hana's Suitcase* is the rebirth of Hana's voice, found and freed by George, Fumiko, and Karen and now heard in every corner of the globe. Our feathers, too, are voices, which refuse to be diminished or forgotten or silenced. Like Hana's, each voice bears witness to the unspeakable horrors of the past and the infinite power we have to determine our future.

Wendy Alexis,
St. Luke Catholic School,
Ottawa, Ontario

One of Karen's cherished mementos is a feather necklace made and given to her by the students at St. Luke.

Grade 6 students at St. Luke Catholic School organize the thousands of donated feathers kept in the steamer trunk. Each feather will be a leaf on the "Angels' Tree," representing someone who perished in the Rwandan genocide.

Reflections

Karen, Fumiko, and George have received thousands of poems and pieces of prose from readers of all age groups.

Students at Henderson Avenue Public School in Thornhill, Ontario produced dramatic letters from "George" and "Hana" telling the outside world about their plight.

Hana and Erika

Two girls.
Separated by time.
Two mops of hair,
Two pairs of eyes,
Two loving families,
Two warm homes.
Hana and Erika.
Two religions,
Two towns,
Two countries.
Two different times.
One wish;
To be with family.
One got her desire,
The other did not.
She was frozen in time.
Not able to move onward.
Not able to have children.
Not able to tell her own tale.
Now there is only one girl.
Separated by time.
Never to meet.
Hana and Erika.

by Erika, Trenton, Ontario

Life in a Suitcase
Dark brown suitcase
Tattered on the edges
Few words: Hana Brady
Young girl
High spirits
Big dreams
Overflowing love
Family devotion
Strong family ties
A last embrace of Mother's arms
Abundant tears
Dreaded fear as Father leaves
Sadness beyond compare
Few left to care
Empty heart sinking
Left everything she once had
To a society full of horror
An 11th birthday
Celebrated with the stub of a candle
And a few candies
No sweetness
Wishes vanished
Leaving George incomplete
And a tattered suitcase to carry on

by Marnie, West Bloomfield, Michigan

Martha, age 12: At the beginning of this year I thought that racism meant bullying or teasing people because they're different. I thought I knew all about it because I witness it almost every day at school. Then I read *Hana's Suitcase* and it opened my eyes to the Holocaust. It made me realize that this kind of terrible hatred, if not suppressed, can result in horrifying crimes. If everyone knew about the tragedy of the Holocaust then maybe we can prevent it from happening again.

Racism

The day started out like all others before,
I got ready for school and went out the door,
And caught the bus with no clue in my head,
The troubles awaiting for me just ahead.

It began just at lunchtime, out on the yard,
Some bullies decided to make someone's life hard.
We gathered to watch them poking and jeering,
Making fun of his glasses, his skin and his clothing.

We watched the cruel scene, some laughed right along,
Not realizing that what we were doing was wrong.
We weren't the culprits, the guilty one
And it was all forgotten after the bell had rung.

Yet, on the way home as I remembered the row,
I thought that maybe I could have defused it somehow.
Had I not just stood, watch them torment their prey
Then a portion of racism could have been abolished that day.

And at that moment something crazy came into my head.
Perhaps if we care a bit more instead,
If we stand up for those victims and fight for their say,
Then maybe all racism can be beaten today.

Journal Response: The Holocaust
By: Winnie

Learning about the Holocaust and about how the Jews were treated makes me think about how lucky I am to be here today; being able to read, go to school, and hang out with friends.

It was the exact opposite for the Jews; they were stripped of their families, mistreated, starved, and killed unlawfully.

The way the Jews were murdered was brutal and inhuman; almost as if they were animals instead of people. Tattooed, shaved, stripped— they were imprisoned, kept for work, and slaughtered. Yet, people were still able to survive. I'm amazed at those people. To survive what they went through, I think, would take a lot of courage, smarts, and miracles.

"I can't believe that really happened," were the words my nine-year-old, Kaylee, spoke after we finished reading the book *Hana's Suitcase*, by Karen Levine. I must admit that the shock and disbelief in her voice echoed a part of my own sentiments toward the horrors of the Holocaust, yet I knew as a mother that it was my responsibility to acknowledge and verify the truth of the words we had just read together.

My only comfort was in knowing that such horrible truths had been placed within a context that I felt would help her understand and cope with such horrors. More specifically, I believe that this book, the true story of young Hana Brady and her family, provided a tough, yet tender context for the Holocaust — one that my daughter and her friends could relate to and better understand. In doing so, this book touched not only our minds, but also our hearts. It is a book that I believe can transform the lives of its readers and hopefully, the future for all.

by Darlene (parent of three children)

Sad and lonely,
In a place like prison,
Without mother, without father,
Life is just a disaster.
Without Hana, my dear sister,
Life is just not the same as before.

A strange place we live in.
Cruel soldiers everywhere,
Watching our every move,
No freedom, no privacy,
Hungry all the time,
For there is not enough food.

I hunger not only for food,
But for freedom and family.

by Peter, Kanata, Ontario

Until I saw Hana's Suitcase
I did not know that genocide was organized extermination of a whole nation.
Or that children would not always go to school.
I never knew that children could be taken away from their parents.
Nor did I know that children would go to concentration camps.
Or that they would go to death camps and have to wait to die.
Until I saw Hana's Suitcase.

by Mandy, Winnipeg, Manitoba

I AM NOT THAT FOND OF HISTORY BUT THIS BOOK WAS EXCELLENT. THERE IS NOTHING THAT I WOULD ADD TO THE BOOK OR TAKE AWAY FROM IT. I WOULD ADVISE EVERYBODY TO READ THIS BOOK BECAUSE THIS IS WHAT COULD HAPPEN AGAIN. NOBODY WOULD HAVE BELIEVED THAT HITLER COULD GET AWAY WITH WHAT HE DID. FORGETTING WHAT HE DID COULD BE OUR WORST CRIME.

by Liza, Toronto, Ontario

Straight from the Heart

Hana

Hana Oh Hana,
You Were Tooken To A Jail.
Where You Starved.

Love

Hana loved her life.
Hana loved her family.
She wanted to live.

Children
Lots of children died.
Children did not want to die.
The war is endless!

by Rebecca

Hana Brady.
Poor sweet Hana was so young when
She was taken to the gas chamber
She was cowragous,

Brittany

War
Nobody wants war
We should try and stop the war
We just hate the war

Bailey

Hana's story has moved even the very youngest readers.

Hana's Song

I read a story
About a young girl
A true story
That changed my world
So many questions
still in my mind
With answers I must find.

Just a small child
In a small Czech town
But such a strong child
When her world came down
But Hana's dreams fell
Like a setting sun
In 1941.

(chorus) A few pictures give me clues
A few faces that she once knew
A few memories that she embraced
In Hana's brown suitcase.

(bridge) A different world
A different place
Something's leading me back
to her innocent face…

I'll have the courage
To let others know
I'll have the courage to let her dreams grow
To share her story and we've just begun to tell
Each and every one.

Words by Ventura Park Grade 8 class and Gregg Lawless. Music by Gregg Lawless. Along with the original radio documentary that inspired the book, you can hear "Hana's Song" on the CD at the end of the book.

Ventura Park's Grade 8 class performs "Hana's Song" accompanied by Gregg Lawless on the guitar.

A Musical Journey

Suitcases imply a journey. Yet when I first began reading *Hana's Suitcase* with a Grade 8 class at Ventura Park Public School, in Thornhill, Ontario, I had no way of knowing what an extraordinary road lay ahead.

The students were multi-ethnic, coming from all parts of the world. Some had seen suffering, experienced prejudice or racism; others had never heard about the Holocaust. And yet, each and every one of these young people found themselves reeled in and ultimately enthralled by Hana's story. The more I read, the more they insisted I keep reading. Very often they wouldn't let me put the book down!

The class became passionate about creating something significant in order to recognize the impact Hana's story had on them. Most importantly, they wanted to share their creation with other students.

And so began the amazing year of our Hana's Suitcase Project, where we produced a traveling suitcase exhibit, met with Holocaust survivors, and created hundreds of works of art and stories. But we still wanted to do more. A significant part of that time was spent creating a song of remembrance honoring Hana. The students spent many hours trying to determine what were the best ways to communicate with people their age and, of course, concluded that music was the route to all children's hearts.

A music consultant, Yana Ioffe, was pulled in and she loved the idea from the get-go. Next, Gregg Lawless, a professional musician, agreed to help the students create an original song. Together they did just that. Everyone was so pleased with the results that we decided to record the effort. We did it in a professional studio! I was able to find a member of the community who thought the project was very special and agreed to cover the cost.

The students loved the process and took enormous pride in having commemorated Hana through their own efforts while sharing what they had learned with so many others. We are all thrilled that Karen, Fumiko, and George are playing our song for audiences all over the world.

—Ilyse Lustig, 2012

Think of Freedom...

Secret art classes were held in Theresienstadt where the Brady children were imprisoned for two years. The teacher told her students to think of space and freedom and to draw what they imagined. Some of Hana's artwork, which is reproduced in the book, is in the Jewish Museum in Prague. Now, seventy years later, children around the world remember Hana and other children of the Holocaust through artwork of their own.

by Bradley, Upper Montclair, New Jersey

Grade 3 students at General Stewart School in Lethbridge, Alberta decorated paper suitcases, each containing their thoughts and feelings about Hana's Suitcase.

by students from Dr. George Weir Elementary School, Vancouver, British Columbia

*During a visit to New Jersey in 2004, a student
named Sam presented Fumiko with his work.*

Freedom

My gift to the Holocaust museum is a portrait of Fumiko and George opening Hana's suitcase and freeing her soul from being forgotten. When Fumiko received the suitcase, she didn't just put it on display. She researched and publicized it until Hana was no longer trapped with her suitcase, the only remnant of her. She is no longer just another number in the 6,000,000 death toll. No. Now Hana's spirit, with the help of George and Fumiko, has been freed to teach others. George and Fumiko are also levitating in the air, because they, too, in a way, are angels. They have done great things, with pure heart, and together have taught many children about the Holocaust. I hope that my portrait teaches children as much as Fumiko, George, and everyone involved in this episode has, and I thank them for bringing this story to me.

by students from Skokie Solomon Schechter Day School, Skokie, Illinois

from A Book of Memories by the Grade 4 class at Gander Academy, Newfoundland

Remembering Hana

Hana's Suitcase

Presented
Skok... ...Grade Students
Skol... ...ter Day Schools
...kie ...nois
Novem... 2003

My dearest one, I wish you all the best on your birthday. I am sorry that I can't help you blow out the candles this year. But the heart is a charm I made for your bracelet. Are your clothes getting too small for you? Ask Daddy and Georgie to speak to your aunts about having some new ones made for my big girl. I think about you and your brother all the time. I am well. Are you being a good girl? Will you write me a letter? I hope you and George are keeping up your studies. I am well. I miss you so much, dearest Hanichka. I am kissing yo now.

Love, Mother May 1941 Ravensbruck

Hannah

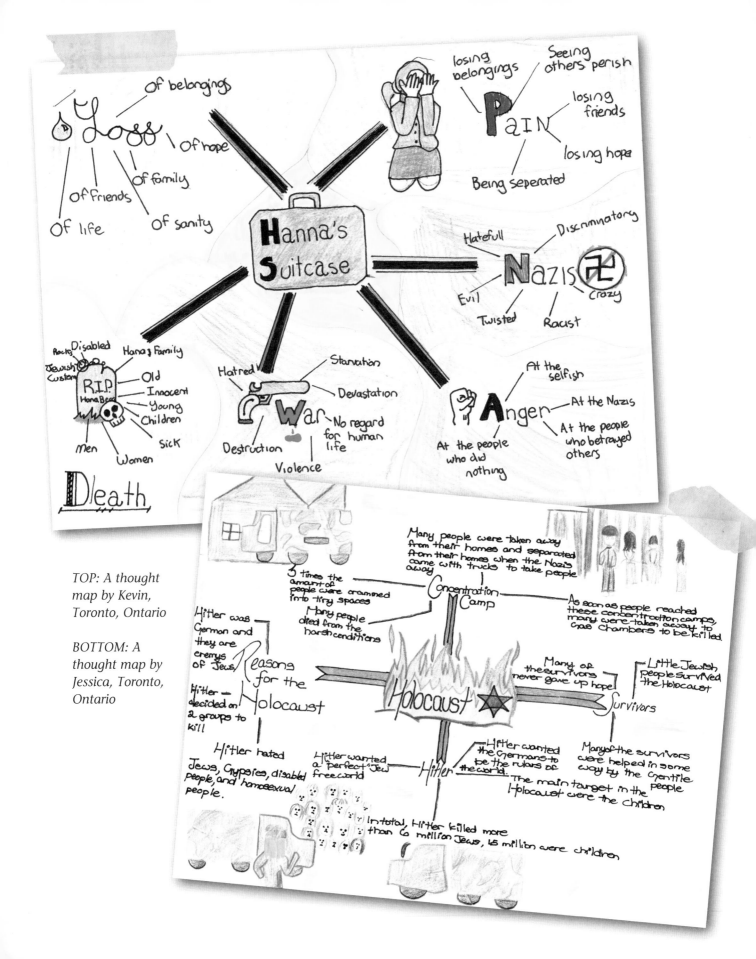

TOP: A thought map by Kevin, Toronto, Ontario

BOTTOM: A thought map by Jessica, Toronto, Ontario

by Brittany, Aurora, Ontario

by William, Pleasantville, New York

Think of Space....

Ilan Ramon, Israel's first astronaut, wrote the diary entry below shortly before embarking on the final mission of the space shuttle Columbia *in 2003.*

He had just finished reading Hana's Suitcase *and was profoundly touched by it. On that fateful shuttle mission, to honor his own relatives who died in the Holocaust, Ilan Ramon carried a drawing by Peter Ginz, a talented Jewish boy George knew at Theresienstadt, and who died at Auschwitz. It was a picture of what the earth would look like from the moon.*

On February 1, 2003, on its way home, Columbia *exploded. Ilan Ramon and all six other crew members perished.*

We cherish his words.

"I just finished reading the book *Hana's Suitcase*. It is hard to avoid the thought that it happened less than sixty years ago. You look at Hana's photograph, a beautiful, innocent girl, and you can not understand how and why...

"...Hana's story is incredibly related to the story of Peter Ginz, who was probably at the same place in Theresienstadt. He may have taken drawing lessons with Hana's teacher and maybe that teacher inspired Peter to draw the painting 'Landmoon Scape.' As it is written in the book, the teacher instructed the children to think about space, about freedom, and let their imaginations lead them to draw whatever came to their minds.

"There is almost no doubt in my mind that Hana's and Peter's stories are …intertwined. Maybe both of them even rode the same horrible train from Theresienstadt to Auschwitz and were led on the same day from the platform to the gas chambers. It is hard to stop the tears when you read the story and [have] the feeling of responsibility to go on and tell the story, to educate our children and the children of the world about the horrors of the Holocaust.

"Maybe I am oversensitive because I am second generation [survivor], and I am strongly connected to the Holocaust. I've made up my mind that after I come back from space, I will join the youth in the 'March of the Living' to Auschwitz. I feel I must be there."

Ilan Roman
Shabbat, October 23, 2002

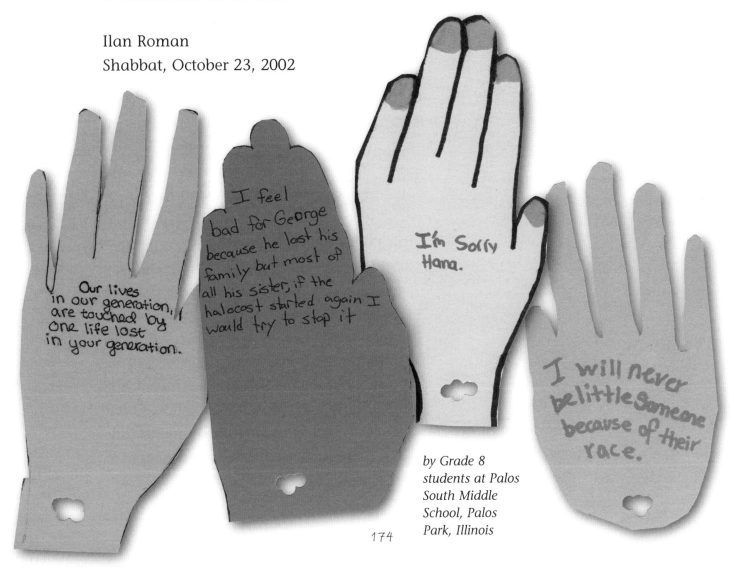

Our lives in our generation, are touched by one life lost in your generation.

I feel bad for George because he lost his family but most of all his sister, if the halocost started again I would try to stop it

I'm Sorry Hana.

I will never belittle someone because of their race.

by Grade 8 students at Palos South Middle School, Palos Park, Illinois

174